Feb. 10th, 2007

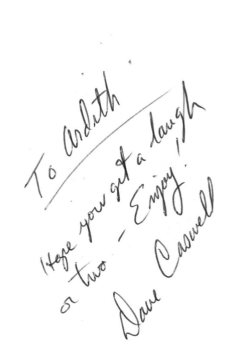

To Ardith
Hope you get a laugh
or two - Enjoy!
Dave Caswell
Dave

Laughter Prevents Wrinkles

A collection of articles and
embellishments about retirement,
aging, kids and general nonsense.
A good chuckle will do you good –
try it!

DAVE CASWELL

Copyright © 2004 by David G. Caswell

ISBN 0-7414-1992-0

Published by:

INFINITY
PUBLISHING.COM

1094 New Dehaven Street
Suite 100
West Conshohocken, PA 19428-2713
Info@buybooksontheweb.com
www.buybooksontheweb.com
Toll-free (877) BUY BOOK
Local Phone (610) 520-2500
Fax (610) 519-0261

∞

Printed in the United States of America

Printed on Recycled Paper

Published April 2004

ACKNOWLEDGMENTS:

As expected, I'd like to acknowledge my parents, my wife, our four sons and our grandkids, my barber and the man who cleans our pool. Actually, none of these people had a damn thing to do with this book – but they have been acknowledged anyway. Lastly and seriously, I want to give thanks to my God for giving me a sense of humor and the ability to share it.

Dave Caswell

Green Valley, Arizona
&
Pinetop, Arizona
Spring 2004

* * * * * * *

"SURE – LET'S GET MARRIED"

The two couples had known each other and had been best friends for over fifty years. Within a few months of each other, Hank's wife and Ann's husband passed away. The two surviving spouses stayed in Green Valley and found great comfort in each other's company. In fact, they did everything together. They went to the movies, out to dinner; they played golf together, went to parties as a couple and thoroughly enjoyed the companionship they were having. After almost a year, Hank said to Ann one evening, "You know what Ann; I've been thinking you and I should get married." Ann didn't have to think about the proposal for only a short minute and replied, "Sure, why not? We have known each other for over fifty years and we both get along and enjoy each other's company. Yes, Hank, I think it's a good idea." Pausing for a moment, she continued, "but, if we do get married, there are three things I want." "Okay with me, honey. What are the three things?" "Well, first of all Hank, I want to keep my own car so that I can come and go as I please – you know, so you won't have to drive me around." Hank said, "Fine with me. Consider it done. What's number two?" "Number two is that I want my own personal checking account. As you know, my husband, God rest his soul, left me some money and I'd like to be independent with my money." Hank again replied, "I fully understand and I agree. You shall have your

own checking account. What's number three?"
Now Ann paused a bit and began to blush.
Hank said, "Go ahead sweetheart, what is it?"
"Oh Hank, this is kind of embarrassing, but
okay, here goes. Hank, I'm used to having sex
three times a week – every Monday, Wednesday and Friday." "Ann, honey, I see no real
problem with that. Let's see now – why don't
you put me down for Wednesdays."

* * * * * * *

Blessed are they who can laugh at themselves
for they shall never cease to be amused.

* * * * * * *

My life's guiding rule has always been, "You are
only young once but you can always be imma-
ture." If we can't have some fun and laugh at
ourselves once and awhile, this old world would
be a pretty sad place.

K – I – N – K –Y

My wife and I retired to Green Valley, Arizona, from Wisconsin. We bought a beautiful lot in a new subdivision and designed what would be our new home. Because we like open space and lots of glass, we planned the layout so that most every room would have a spectacular view of the Santa Rita Mountains. Did I say every room – yes - Our master bath has an eight-foot sliding glass door right in front of the shower and the toilet.

Every day during construction, Luke, the love-able lab and I would drive up to the building site to check on the progress and take a nice walk. When the new house was about two-thirds finished, we parked in the cul-de-sac and noticed an unfamiliar couple coming out of the house. As you know, it's common for people to go into a house under construction – just to check it out. Snooping is permissible – up to a point.

After we exchanged pleasantries, they asked me, "Have you been in this new house?" I said I had wondered through it on occasion. The strangers looked at each other, then at me and the husband said, "Did you notice that whoever is building this place is going to have a large glass door right in front of the toilet. How weird can you get?" Not telling them that it was my house I said, "Ya, I guess you could call it weird." But his wife hadn't given her opinion yet. She said with hands on hips, "Weird, I'd call it kinky." Finally, I asked where they were from. "Portland, Oregon," they replied and asked where I lived. I said, "Right here – this is our new home."

Well, the husband turned and walked to their car without another word. His wife however couldn't let well enough alone. She had to open mouth and insert foot even further. She stammered rather embarrassingly and said in an apologetic way, "You know, it's a lovely new home. Do you know how I'd describe that glass door in the master bath? I'd call it very <u>unique</u>." I said with a straight face, "No ma'am, not unique. We wanted the KINKY look."

As she turned to go to their car, she uttered her one word response, "Sick."

* * * * * *

I believe the only time the world beats a path to my door is when I'm in the bathroom.

TIME TO GET UP; HERE'S YOUR SQUASH

You have heard the expression, "Bringing home the bacon," but have you ever heard of "Bringing home the squash?" Luke, the loveable lab, and I walk every morning about the time dawn is breaking. On our daily walk, Luke picks up everything that's not permanently attached to the earth.

One of Luke's good friends is Rocky, a lab mix. The two of them greet each other and then we're on our way. His second friend that we see is Bentley. Bentley is a typical, droopy-faced beagle hound. They greet each other in a very laid-back, relaxed manner – you can't get too excited when you're around Bentley. His third good friend is Bob-the-Dog. BTD, as we call him, is a true Heinz 57. Some mornings BTD is still in his house, and Luke and I hurry on past. Who really needs BTD at that hour?

It was a beautiful winter morning in Pinetop and Luke and I were moving right along when suddenly Luke spotted a foreign object over in the snow bank. He nearly pulled my arm out of the socket as he lunged to retrieve this valuable treasure. By the dim early morning light, I could see that whatever it was, it wasn't alive and it didn't make noises. Still, I wasn't sure I wanted to take it out of Luke's mouth. He looked up as if to say, "This is a wonderful thing. Here, take a look."

"Oh for heaven's sakes, I should have known all along that it was a large, firm, green acorn squash. How silly of me, Luke. I should have expected you to find a perfectly good squash here in the snow bank."

With squash in mouth and jaw locked, we cut our walk short. I got the message right away. We were going home to show Sleeping Beauty, my wife, what we had found. OOPS, here comes Rocky. Luke looked up and said out of the corner of his mouth, "Let's keep right on walking." I don't want to take time to monkey around with him." In the next block, who should be standing by his driveway but old sobersides, Bentley. Again, Luke made no apologies for not wanting to stop – we were on a mission and Bentley didn't fit into Luke's plans.

As we got back home and quietly opened the door, I could tell that my wife wasn't out of bed yet. The hallway was dark and no lights were on in the bathroom. This did not alter Luke's plans. Down the hall and into the bedroom with the most fantastic squash any lab has ever found. Just as little Miss Sunshine was swinging her legs out of bed, Luke deposited his snow-covered squash in her nightie-covered lap. Well, let me tell you—talk about a Kodak moment. It was not a pretty picture. Being presented with a snow-covered squash before your feet hit the floor is probably way down on her list of favorite ways to be awakened. As Luke and I retreated, he looked up and said, "She has no sense of humor at all."

* * * * * *

The trouble with some women is that they get all excited about nothing and then they marry him.

* * * * * *

Always stare at nudists—it's not a sin.

* * * * * *

Bill: I think she married me for my money.
Dan: Well, she earned it.

OLD "YOUNG" LOVE

An elderly couple was celebrating their 50th wedding anniversary, so they decided to return to the little town where they first met. They sat in a small coffee shop in the town and were telling the waitress about their love for each other and how they met at this same spot. Sitting in the next booth was the local cop and he smiled as the old couple spoke.

After the waitress left the table, the old man said to his wife, "Remember the first time we made love? It was up in that field across the road, when I put you against the fence. Why don't we do it again for old time's sake?" The wife giggled and said, "Sure, why not."

So, off they went out the door and across to the field. The cop smiled to himself, thinking how romantic this was and decided he better keep an eye on the couple so they didn't run into any harm.

The old couple walked to the field and as they approached the fence, they began to undress. The old man picked up his wife when they were naked and leaned her against the fence. The cop watched from the bushes and was surprised at what he saw. With the vitality of youth, the wife bounced around excitedly, while the husband thrashed around like a wild man, then they both fell to the ground in exhaustion.

Eventually, they stood up, shook themselves, and got dressed. As they walked back towards the road, the cop stepped from his hiding spot and said, "That is the most wonderful love making I have ever seen. You must have been a wild couple when you were young."

"Not really," said the old man. "When we were young, that fence wasn't electric."

* * * * * *

A retiree went to his doctor complaining about a pain in his left knee. The doc said, "I think its old age." The man replied, "Baloney. My right knee is the same age and it feels fine."

* * * * * *

Now that I have hit the age of 70, my wife says that my memory is much shorter and my stories are much longer. Oh ya, the truth does hurt.

NOW HE KNOWS WHETHER
OR NOT HE CAN SING

There are some things in this world I'm sure I will never learn, let alone master. After all, with age you are supposed to come to the realization that you can't do certain things with ease or grace.

For example, I now know I can't draw a person on a piece of paper without it looking like a reindeer. I know I can't play any musical instrument – well, OK, I do play a mean pie tin with two kitchen knives. I've been told I dance like an ostrich with an orthopedic problem. I have never been able to shoot a bow and arrow and hit anything but the ground. I'm fully aware that I'm not an accomplished carpenter, electrician or plumber. I've confessed that if it can't be fixed with duct tape, it stays broken until I can get a neighbor to stop by.

Now, I have to admit to something I did in a moment of weakness. You'd think a person of normal intelligence would have learned from the Marine Corps that you never – I mean never – volunteer for anything. Well, I fell prey to a very persuasive and spunky choir director named Lynn. Yes, I volunteered to become a member of the bass section of the men's church choir. Let me say right up front – I don't read or understand a note of music. I don't know a sharp from a smooth or a flat from a round. A pause to me means taking a 10-minute break, a staff is what the shepherds used to carry and a tenor is half of $20.

This very lovely female choir director told me that this was strictly a 24-hour singing project. Heck, I can fake anything for 24 hours.

I got to our one and only practice Saturday morning and was told in a very clever and cunning way, "Welcome to our new men's choir. You all are charter members of this wonderful and ongoing men's choral group."

Now listen to this. After we sang the first verse, the men standing near me said such reassuring things as, "You certainly have a ... a ... distinctive voice." Another asked, "Did you ever sing in a choir before?" These comments didn't really bother me because I figured they were joking around. However, I started to wonder when one of the men said, "Bet your wife can sing." Another said, "Aren't you usually an usher?"

This one fellow named Warren came to my rescue. Warren started telling me in a very kind way, "Cazzy, see those small round black dots? They are the notes we are supposed to be singing." I quickly traded positions with another bass member so that I could stand next to Warren. Actually, I wasn't just standing next to him, I was leaning against him so that I could hear every note he sang. It didn't take me too long to realize that the term "anchor" has two meanings. A person can be called an anchor, especially if others have to drag him along. On the other hand, an anchor can be a good singer named Warren. I listened to every sound he made and, by golly; I was one-tenth of a second behind him all the way. I have to admit it was fun. If we sing the same hymn for the next couple of years, I'll have it down pat.

Do you think it was pure coincidence that our pastor preached that Sunday morning that the Lord has given each of us special and unique talents? Why did I have the feeling he was talking directly to me?

Maybe my God-given talent is ushering.

* * * * * * *

An optimist is a parent who lets his son borrow the car for a date. A pessimist is one who won't. A cynic is one who did.

ALL SHAPES AND SIZES

Not too long ago my 93-year-old father came from Wisconsin to visit us in Green Valley. One Sunday we took him to our church for the 10:15 AM service. I wanted to get to church early in order to get a front pew seat so that Dad could hear the sermon and see the flowers on the alter. We were able to get a perfect seat in the front because, as you may know, Lutherans ALWAYS sit in the back of the church.

I had forgotten that this particular Sunday morning we were going to receive communion. Being able to take communion was great because that would give Dad a chance to see how we distributed the bread and wine in our church. As the worshipers came forward down the center isle to kneel at the alter rail, we had a birds eye view of the young and the old, the large and the small and the variety of dress, which in the warmer weather is most often casual. Anyway, as we sat there only a few feet away from the communicants, my Dad leaned over and said in an extremely loud voice, "Say Dave; they sure do come in all shapes and sizes, don't they?" Well, everyone around us started to chuckle. The folks who were kneeling directly in front of us didn't think it was so funny and as they returned to their seats, they directed some harsh looks in our direction. Dad never noticed. At 93 years of age, he was just telling (yelling) it like it is.

* * * * * *

Back when our sons were in school, I remember telling one of our boys that I was worried about his being at the bottom of his class. "Don't worry, Dad," he said. "They teach the same stuff at both ends."

* * * * * *

HANG ON DAD

At a local supermarket, a woman noticed a man pushing a cart down the aisle with a screaming baby in it. The man kept repeating softly, "Don't scream Albert, don't yell, Albert, don't cry, Albert. Keep calm, Albert. Hang on, Buddy." "Excuse me, sir," the woman said, "you certainly are to be commended for so patiently calming little Albert." "Lady," the man explained, "I'm Albert."

THE BEST FROM CHURCH BULLETINS

- Don't let worry kill you – let the church help.

- Thursday night: Potluck supper. Prayer and medication to follow.

- Remember in prayer the many that are sick of our church and community.

- For those of you who have children and don't know it, we have a nursery down stairs.

- The rosebud on the altar this morning is to announce the birth of David Alan Boxer, the sin of Rev. and Mrs. Julius Boxer.

- This afternoon there will be a meeting in the South and North ends of the church. Children will be baptized at both ends.

- Tuesday at 4:00 PM there will be an ice cream social. All ladies giving milk will please come early.

- Wednesday, the ladies' "Liturgy Society" will meet. Mrs. Jones will sing, "Put Me in My Little Bed" accompanied by the pastor.

- Thursday at 5:00 PM there will be a meeting of the Little Mothers Club. All wishing to become little mothers, please see the minister in his study.

- This being Easter Sunday, we will ask Mrs. Lewis to come forward and lay an egg on the altar.

- The service will close with "Little Drops of Water." One of the ladies will start and the rest of the congregation will join in.

- Next Sunday a special collection will be taken to defray the cost of the new carpet. All those wishing to do something on the new carpet will come forward and do so.

- The ladies of the church have cast off clothing of every kind and they may be seen in the church basement Friday.

- A bean supper will be held on Tuesday evening in the church hall. Music will follow.

- At the evening service tonight, the sermon topic will be "What is Hell?" Come early and listen to our choir practice.

- The senior choir invites any member of the congregation who enjoys sinning to join the choir.

- Scouts are saving aluminum cans, bottles and other items to be recycled. Proceeds will be used to cripple children.

- The Lutheran men's group will meet at 6 PM. Steak, mashed potatoes, green beans, bread and dessert will be served for a nominal feel.

- Please place your donation in the envelope along with the decreased person(s) you want remembered.

- Attend and you will hear an excellent speaker and heave a healthy lunch.

- This evening at 7 PM there will be a hymn sing in the park across from the Church. Bring a blanket and come prepared to sin.

- Ladies Bible Study will be held Thursday morning at 10. All ladies are invited to lunch in the Fellowship Hall after the B.S. is done.

- The pastor would appreciate it if the ladies of the congregation would lend him their electric girdles for the pancake breakfast next Sunday morning.

- Low Self Esteem Support Group will meet Thursday at 7 PM. Please use the back door.

- The eighth graders will be presenting Shakespeare's Hamlet in the Church basement Friday at 7 PM. The Congregation is invited to attend this tragedy.

- Weight Watchers will meet at 7 PM at the First Presbyterian Church. Please use large double door at the side entrance.

- Mrs. Johnson will be entering the hospital this week for testes.

- The Associate Minister unveiled the church's new tithing campaign slogan last Sunday: "I Upped My Pledge. Up Yours."

- Bertha Belch, a missionary from Africa will be speaking tonight at Calvary Memorial Church in Tucson. Come tonight and hear Bertha Belch all the way from Africa.

- Announcement in the church bulleting for a National PRAYER & FASTING Conference: "The cost for attending the Fasting and Prayer conference includes meals."

- Our youth basketball team is back in action Wednesday at 8 PM in the recreation hall. Come out and watch us kill Christ the King.

- Miss Charlene Smith sang, "I will not pass this way again," giving obvious pleasure to the congregation.

- Ladies, don't forget the rummage sale. It's a chance to get rid of those things not worth keeping around the house. Don't forget your husbands.

- The peacemaking meeting scheduled for today has been canceled due to a conflict.

- The sermon this morning: "Jesus Walks on the Water". The sermon tonight: "Searching for Jesus."

- Next Thursday there will be tryouts for the choir. They need all the help they can get.

- Barbara remains in the hospital and needs blood donors for more transfusions. She is also having trouble sleeping and request tapes of Pastor Jack's sermons.

- The Rector will preach his farewell message after which the choir will sing "Break Forth into Joy".

- Irving Benson and Jessie Carter were married on October 24 in the church. So ends a friendship that began in their school days.

* * * * * * *

Never chant while you're drunk—you may say things that aren't appropriate.

* * * * * * *

WHEN YOU GOTTA GO

This summer we went to a wedding on a hot, sticky, long afternoon. The cute little girl, dressed like a doll, carried the silk pillow on which the two wedding rings were placed. She stood patiently for a long time waiting for her moment in the ceremony when the minister would ask for the rings to be exchanged. At that magic moment when he nodded for the little girl to bring the rings, she said in a loud voice for everyone to hear, "I have to go potty."

Ain't life great?

* * * * * * *

By the time you can make ends meet, they move the ends.

* * * * * * *

Reincarnation might be true, but some people should never have been carnated in the first place.

BETTER WRITE IT DOWN

Harry and Lynn were sitting in the front room one evening watching TV. During a commercial Harry said to his wife, "I'm going out to the kitchen for a cookie and a cup of coffee. Can I get you anything, dear?" Lynn replied, "Well, as long as you're up, you could get me a dish of ice cream. That would be nice. But remember our little talk about our failing memories? We agreed that from now on we would write everything down so that we wouldn't forget." Harry replied, "Oh for heaven sakes, Lynn, I surely can remember a simple thing like a dish of ice cream while I'm in the kitchen."

"Well, okay, and while you're in the refrigerator why not put some whip cream on top of the ice cream. Better write it down, honey."

"Lynn, is that all you want?"

"Oh heck, put some of those nuts on top of the Sunday if you don't mind. Sure you don't need to write it down?"

Out to the kitchen Harry went to fetch the treats. Lynn could hear him rummaging around and taking his good old time. After what seemed to be 20 or 30 minutes, Harry returned to the living room with a tray of beautifully prepared bacon, eggs and toast. As he set it down on the table next to Lynn's chair, she said, "See Harry. I told you that you should have written it down. I specifically said I wanted whole-wheat toast.

* * * * * *

You know you're getting old when it's the doctors and not the police who warn you to slow down.

* * * * * *

Going to church doesn't make you a Christian any more than going to a garage makes you a mechanic.

* * * * * *

Distinguished looking: the last stage.

HELLO, WELCOME TO THE PSYCHIATRIC HOTLINE

- If you are obsessive-compulsive, please press 1 repeatedly.

- If you are co-dependent, please ask someone to press 2.

- If you have multi-personalities, please press 3, 4, 5 and 6.

- If you are paranoid-delusional, we know who you are and what you want. Just stay on the line so we can trace the call.

- If you are schizophrenic, listen carefully and a little voice will tell you which number to press.

- If you are manic-depressive, it doesn't matter which number you press. No one will answer.

* * * * * * *

Drink plenty of water and coffee and beer and enjoy life.

THANK GOD FOR TOILET TANKS

As Paul Harvey used to say, "Don't worry. Nothing's going to turn out alright." Not long ago I took a business trip. I was picked up at the airport in Philly and driven to a beautiful small town about an hour away. There was going to be a very important meeting with a big client the next morning. Our representative out East had made hotel reservations for me in the most elegant, historic and extremely expensive accommodations I'd ever stayed in. I mean, we're talking $200 plus per night for a single.

I checked in, had a nice dinner and turned in early because we had to be sharp for our breakfast meeting. I put in a wake-up call for six a.m. – plenty of time to get ready and meet our guests promptly at 7:30.

My phone rang at six a.m. on the dot. After shaving, I was ready to hit the shower, gold fixtures and all. There was even a comfortable seat in the large shower. The bar of soap was large enough for a family of six and the shampoo had a sexy-sounding French name. I thought to myself, "It don't get much better than this."

Without going into detail, I'll just tell you that I was fully lathered from head to toe. I had more suds than a commercial laundry. At just the point of maximum lather, the water went off. Not a drop was coming from the worthless gold showerhead. I was confident, however, that this was only a temporary situation so I stood—eyes closed—getting colder by the minute. Finally, it was desperation time; an executive decision had to be made. I stepped out of the shower and made my soapy way to the telephone. "What do you mean the water will be off for two or three hours until they can fix the broken water main?" I followed my expensive trail of suds back to the bathroom, took the top off the toilet tank, got the drinking glass and one glassful at a time, I sparingly and strategically tried to rinse off.

When they describe bath towels as "thirsty," I put that claim to the ultimate test. I figured that with my toilet tank rinse, plus the use of every towel and washcloth in the room, I got 75% of the suds off. It was with only minutes to spare that I walked into the lobby to meet our guests. I'm sure everyone at our table thought I had some rare muscular disease because I started to itch, and the smell of French shampoo was starting to overtake that part of the restaurant. Not even my Old Spice aftershave could win the war of fragrances. I thought to myself, "If I start to sweat, I know the suds will reappear and I'll sit here looking like the Michelin Man."

After a most uncomfortable day, I couldn't wait to get to my new motel and get into the shower. I stood under the hot water that night; the lather literally flowed out of every pore. Oh, by the way, we did close the business deal.

* * * * * *

MEMORY MEDICINE

A friend tells the delightful story about the elderly gentleman who called on one of his old friends and opened the conversation with a customary, "Well, what's new?"

"Well," replied the old timer, "the best news is that great new medication I'm taking to improve my memory."

"You don't say," responded the visitor. "I could use some of that myself. What's the name of it?"

There was a pause before the old man said, "What's the name of the red flower that grows on a bush with thorns?" "A rose?" "Yeah, that's it," exclaimed the old man as he turned toward the kitchen and called out, "Hey, Rose! What the heck is the name of that medication I'm taking for my memory?"

SURPRISE – SISTER

Two elderly sisters were driving up to Tucson one day. As they got into heavier traffic, Edna noticed that her older sister drove right through a red light. She didn't say anything, but as they went along her sister drove directly through another red traffic light. This same thing happened a third and a fourth time. Finally, Doris turned to Edna and said, "Sister you have driven through several red lights. We could have had a bad accident." Edna replied, "Oh good heavens, am I driving?"

* * * * * * *

As one of our neighbors said, "If you have given up trying to open something, tell a four-year-old not to touch it. Works every time."

* * * * * * *

There's no task so difficult that a little hard work and a lot of shifting the blame won't solve

* * * * * * *

Nine out of 10 homemakers agree: The best way to remove cooking odors is to quit cooking.

AILMENTS

A group of senior citizens in Green Valley, Arizona, was exchanging notes about their ailments.

"My arm is so weak I can hardly hold this coffee cup."

"Yes, I know. My cataracts are so bad I can't see to pour the coffee."

"I can't turn my head because of the arthritis in my neck."

"My blood pressure pills make me dizzy."

"I guess that's the price we pay for getting old."

"Well, it's not all bad. We should be thankful that we can still drive here in Green Valley.

* * * * * *

TRIVIA TESTS

We Americans are trivia nuts. If you want to fire up a dinner table conversation, just casually ask, "Does anyone know what percent of the US population are <u>real</u> blondes?" Or, you could ask, "What do you think the most commonly used word in the English language is? How about the second most used word?" (I suppose I should tell you the correct answers to these first couple of questions before we go on to the freshman level: 16% of our population are real blondes. "The" is the most commonly used word, and "of" is second.) While doing these questions, you may want to slide a piece of paper down the page so you don't see the answers right away.

Q. Sunlight takes 8 minutes to get here. How long does it take moonlight?

A. 1.3 seconds.

Q. According to sleep researchers, how long does it take the average person to fall asleep at night?

A. 7 minutes.

Q. Are bald or balding men in the minority or majority in the U.S.?

A. Majority – 60%.

Q. Who was the first person to fly an airplane solos in Australia?

A. None other than Harry Houdini.

Q. How long do you think a golfer has to wait to book a starting time on Scotland's St? Andrews Old Course?

A. Six months.

Q. If you had a "circumorbital hematoma", what would you have?

A. A black eye.

Q. If you ordered "Paste of Fat Liver", what would you be getting?

A. Pate de Foie Gras.

Q. What is a "biggin?"

A. The coffeepot's perforated basket for grounds.

Q. The onion is the national flower of what country?

A. Wales (actually it's a leek, but who cares anyway?)

Q. Mix white paint into red, you get a tint. Mix black paint into red, you get a shade.

What do you get if you mix both white and black into red?

A. A tone.

Q. Is "Whistler's Mother" an American painting?

A. No. The painting was painted in England, owned by France since 1891, and is now in the Louvre.

Q. Satchel Paige at age 47 was the oldest baseball player to play in an All-Star game. Who was the youngest?

A. Dwight Gooden at 19.

Q. What's the third most commonly spoken language in Houston, Texas?

A. Vietnamese.

Q. Name 6 animals that produce ivory?

A. Elephant, walrus, whale, elk, hippo and boar.

Q. How did the saying, "That's the ticket" get started?

A. It started out as "That's the etiquette."

Q. What two islands in the British Empire have no snakes?

A. Ireland and Montserrat in the British West Indies.

Q. True or False: It takes the same energy to walk in high heels as it does to walk in flats.

A. 65% more energy to walk in high heels. (False)

Q. If Rhode Island is the smallest state, what's the second smallest?

A. Delaware.

Q. What kind of animal is a "hob?"

A. A male ferret; a female is a "jill."

Q. Do horses yawn?

A. No. Neither do cows, goats or sheep—only meat-eating mammals yawn.

Q. Do more people fall up or down the stairs?

A. Upstairs.

Q. Do elephants lie down to sleep?

A.   Baby elephants do; adults do only occasionally.

Q.   Why do 29% of murders by women occur in the kitchen?

A.   That's where the butcher knives are.

* * * * * * *

I read this article that said the typical symptoms of stress are: eating too much, impulse buying, and driving too fast. Are they kidding? That's my idea of a perfect day.

* * * * * * *

A duck walked into the drugstore and said to the pharmacist, "May I have a tube of lip balm, please?" The druggist smirked, "What are you going to do with lip balm? You have no money and you have no lips." "Never mind," the duck said. "Just put it on my bill."

A WOMAN'S RANDOM THOUGHTS

Reasons to smile:

- Every 7 minutes of every day, someone in an aerobics class pulls a hamstring.

- Women over 50 don't have babies because they would put them down and forget where they left them.

- One of life's mysteries is how a 2-pound box of candy can make a woman gain 5 pounds.

- My mind not only wanders, it sometimes leaves completely.

- The best way to forget all your troubles is to wear tight shoes.

- The nice part about living in a small town is that when you don't know what you're doing, someone else does.

- The older you get, the tougher it is to lose weight because by then, your body and your fat are really good friends.

- Amazing! You hang something in your closet for a while and it shrinks two sizes!

- Skinny people irritate me! Especially when they say things like, "You know, sometimes I just forget to eat." Now I've forgotten my address, my mother's maiden name, and my keys. But, I've never forgotten to eat.

- A friend of mine confused her Valium with her birth control pills. She had 14 kids, but she doesn't really care.

- If you love something, set it free. If it comes back, it will always be yours.

  o If it doesn't come back, it was never yours to begin with. But, if it just sits in your living room, messes up your stuff, eats your food, uses your telephone, takes your money, and doesn't appear to realize that you had set it free... you either married it or gave birth to it.

* * * * * * *

It's a narrow mind that can only figure out one way to spell a word.

A SUREFIRE STRESS-FREE DIET

Weight is a relative thing. I seem to notice it first on my relatives. Looking back over the years, it's interesting how our human nature allows us to rationalize lots of things. In high school and in college, I vowed I would never get out of shape. In the good old USMC, I promised myself I would always be able to run the obstacle course. We had four sons and I was confident, several years ago, that I would always be able to beat them in a foot race, or in a wrestling match. Well, my friends, it ain't so.

Hopefully, with age comes experience, wisdom, common sense, a little mellowness (and grandkids). Not so welcome are the eyeglasses, the forgetfulness and the pounds. The weight seems to come and go – depending on the time of year, our social calendar and comments from family and friends. But as time goes by, the pounds come-and-stay instead of come-and-go.

I'll share some of my tricks with you; please be discreet with this information. When you buy a pair of new pants or a new belt, always get them at least two sizes too large. Don't worry about the pleats – it's worth the peace of mind knowing what you're doing is right. I also buy full-cut shirts and bulky sweaters – they hid a multitude of sins. Thirdly, I'll share my new Stress-Free Diet with you. Try it – you'll like it!

CAZZY'S STRESS-FREE DIET

BREAKFAST:

½ grapefruit, 1 piece dry, whole-wheat toast

8 oz. Skim milk

LUNCH:

4 oz lean broiled chicken breast, 1 c steamed zucchini, 1 Oreo cookie

Herb tea

AFTERNOON SNACK:

Remainder of Oreo cookies in package, 1-quart Rocky Road ice cream

1 jar hot fudge

DINNER:

1 loaf of toasted garlic bread, 1 large mushroom and pepperoni pizza

1 pitcher of beer and 3 Milky Ways

BEDTIME SNACK

I frozen cheesecake eaten directly from freezer

NOTE: On weekends, you may start with the afternoon snack if you wish.

Don't let those few extra pounds get to you; life is too short to live in fear of good food. Those friends who can eat anything and still look fantastically slim and trim – they're just showing off. I've rationalized this whole thing.

* * * * * *

Thou shalt not weigh more than thy refrigerator.

* * * * * *

A grandkid asked his grandpa, "Can you make a sound like a frog?" Grandpa asks, "Why?" His grandson answered, "Cause Mom and Dad said that when Grandpa croaks we'll be able to go on a cruise."

I LIKE YOUR THINKING

Not long ago on the golf course, I mentioned to my playing partner that this August I will turn seventy. Tom said, "Oh no, don't ever say you're going to be seventy. I have thought about this over the years and I'll tell you what I do. You tell people that you are 69 plus 1. Next year you'll be 69 plus 2 and so on." I liked his idea so well that on the next green I gave him an eight-foot putt. (That gave him a seven on that hole.) I hope he'll give me an eight-foot putt when I'm 69 plus 16.

* * * * * * *

LAUGHING DOG

Not long ago my travels took me to Boston. One rainy evening I had nothing to do, so I went to the movies. After buying my ticket and making my way into the dark theater, I realized I was sitting behind a young woman and her collie dog. At humorous parts in the movie, the dog would laugh with delight and was obviously having a wonderful time. As the movie ended, I could stand it no longer. "Pardon me," I said politely. "I couldn't help but notice your dog. Imagine him laughing like that, enjoying himself so much." "I'm just as amazed as you are," she responded. "He hated the book."

OLD TIMERS HAVE FUN WITH
CITY SLICKERS

When I was a kid, I can remember going deer hunting up north with my dad and the "Older guys." I'll never forget one story that was told around the potbelly stove. It seems there was a weathered old gal named Bertha. She could whip most any man in town, and word was that she shaved every morning. Bertha could "chaw a cud of tobacco" with the best of them. This crusty ol' gal got her deer every year and never fired a shot. Bertha would sit behind a tree overlooking the clearing where deer were known to travel. She'd watch and sooner or later a couple of city fellas, all dressed up in their new red outfits, would clunk and crack their way through the woods. Eventually, one of these "slickers" would scare up a doe and as the deer crossed the open meadow, they'd open fire. Bertha would watch and wait until they had labored and sweat and got all messy dressing the deer out and then she'd come storming out of the woods. With a voice like a foghorn, she'd tell them dudes that they had shot an illegal deer. "You two jerks, get the *!#*!# out of here and I never want to see you again or else I'll wrap those fancy rifles around your necks—MOVE!!" Yup, ol' Bertha always had fresh venison in her freezer and never did fire a shot.

HOW MANY SHEEP

Did I ever tell you about the city slicker that approached Grandpa one day out on the back road by his sheep farm? This fella got out of his expensive new van, and asked Grandpa for directions to town. As they passed the time of day, the city fella turned to Grandpa and said with a cocky voice, "Old man, if I can tell you exactly how many sheep you have over there on that hillside, can I keep one?"

Grandpa glanced at the vast field of sheep, eyed the stranger carefully, snickered and then accepted the bet. The stranger looked carefully across the rolling hillside, scanning left and right, and then said, "5279."

"Holy cow!" Grandpa exclaimed, "How did you do that?" "Well, I'd rather not say," answered the city man. "Now can I have my sheep?"

Grandpa sighed, "A deal's a deal, I guess." The stranger picked out an animal and began to lead it toward his van. Grandpa watched in silence for a moment, and then he called after the man. "Wait! If I can guess where you're from, will you give me back my animal?" "Fair enough," the man agreed with a grin. "You're from Chicago," guessed Grandpa.

Instantly the stranger's smile turned to a frown. "How did you know that?" "Well, I'd rather not say," Grandpa, said. "Now, can I have my dog back?"

* * * * * * *

CAN'T TELL A LIE

When Bill was a young boy in northern Wisconsin, he was always getting into trouble. One morning while waiting for the school bus, he pushed the family outhouse into the pond and went off to school as if nothing had happened. When he got home that afternoon, his father was waiting for him. "Son, did you push the outhouse into the pond?" "Yes, father," said Bill. "Like George Washington, I cannot tell a lie." Bill's father took off his belt and said, "All right, son, bend over. I'm going to give you a spanking." Bill tried to explain that Mr. Washington didn't spank George when he admitted chopping down the cherry tree. "Yes, son," said Bill's father, "but George's father wasn't in the cherry tree."

* * * * * * *

Into every life some rain must fall, usually on the day you wash your car.

* * * * * * *

The only book that really tells you where to go on your vacation is your checkbook.

* * * * * * *

LET'S GET YOU UNDRESSED

It all started with the firm written instructions, "Nothing to eat or drink—and that includes water—for three months prior to your lab and x-ray tests." Okay, so I exaggerated a little. I couldn't eat or drink anything for twelve hours prior to my scheduled appointment at the medical clinic. (It just seemed like three months.) I'll have to admit that after brushing my teeth, I did sneak half a swallow of water when I was rinsing my mouth.

I arrived at the clinic at 8:45 a.m. "Please have a seat, Mr. Caswell, and the lab tech will be with you shortly. You haven't had anything to eat or drink, have you?" I couldn't even answer her 'cause my mouth was so dry. Finally, the lady with the sharp fangs called me into her laboratory for the "bloodletting". I'm not a chicken but I never look when she inserts the needle—just one of those times when I'd rather look at all those official-looking diplomas hanging on the wall.

With the white ball of cotton covering the massive hole in the crook of my arm, I headed for Radiology. Again, I was told to have a seat.

"The x-ray tech will be with you shortly." My stomach started rumble, just a reminder that man does not live on lobby magazines dated April 1982 alone. This lovely young lady came into the waiting area, took a patient folder off of the counter and announced, "Mr. David Caswell. Please follow me. Let's get you undressed." As the other people in the waiting room looked up, I couldn't help but respond, "That's the best offer I've had so far today." To which the young x-ray tech responded, "If that's what lights your fire, we're all in trouble."

As I was handed a size SMALL gown and an even shorter bathrobe, my next instructions were to undress, including my shoes and socks, and put the gown on first with the opening in the back and then the robe with the opening in the front. Well, now, let's get real. First of all, I was in this coat closet sized cubical. At 6'4" tall, it's hard enough to contort your way out of your clothes, but now I have to get into this pre-World War I gown. I put my arms through so that the opening was in the back—that's the easy part. Now try to tie those two little strings located somewhere behind your neck. Finally, after several tries to find both strings, I took the damn thing off and pre-tied the strings so that they would go behind my neck and the middle of my back. Now, I'll just slip this whole blasted gown over my head and we'll be all set. Negatory. I had tied the little strings in such nice, neat bows that now I couldn't get my head through the neck opening. "How are you doing in there, Mr. Caswell?"

I quickly untied the silly gown and put it on—then—put the robe on and tied the sash. Talk about a Kodak moment—the robe came down to just above my knees. Oh well – The whole ordeal reminded me of this little ditty:

> I was fluoroscoped and cystoscoped
> My aging frame displayed,
> Stripped upon an ice-cold table,
> While my gizzards were x-rayed.
> I was checked for worms and parasites,
> For fungus and the crud,
> While they pierced me with large needles,
> Taking samples of my blood.
> Doctors came to check me over,
> Probed and pushed and poked around,
> And to make sure that I was living,
> They wired me for sound.
> They have finally concluded,
> Their results have filled the page,
> What I have will someday kill me,
> My affliction is old age.

* * * * * * *

Always remember wrinkles are hereditary. Parents get them from their children.

* * * * * * *

A LITTLE NONSENSE NOW AND THEN

The wisest person relishes a little nonsense now and then. Being sensible all the time and thinking adult thoughts can get very boring. Letting the pressures of the day get to you can, and does, make for a downright stinky existence. It's time to unwind, and I have just the ticket. Here is a letter from a Mom to her son. Go ahead and laugh out loud; see if it doesn't lighten your load.

Dear Son,

I'm writing this slow cause I know you don't read real fast. Your dad and I moved; we don't live where we did when you left for the big city. Your dad read in the paper that most accidents happen within 20 miles of home, so we moved.

Honey, the coat you wanted me to send to you – well, Aunt Norma said she thought it would be a little heavy to send in the mail with them big, heavy buttons and all, so we cut the buttons off and put them in the pocket. You should get the coat soon.

We got a letter from the funeral home, said if we didn't make the last payment on Grandma's funeral by the end of the month, up she comes. Speaking of funerals, son – your second uncle Dick fell in the whiskey vat. Some men from down the street tried to pull him out but he fought them off and, by golly, he drowned. We had him cremated – burned for just over three days.

About your sister, Sue. She had a baby early this morning. I haven't found out yet if it's a boy or a girl so I don't know if you are an aunt or an uncle. We'll go over to the hospital this morning and let you know by the weekend.

A bit of bad news to report. It seems your three high school friends, David, Ed and Cole, went off the Wilson Road Bridge in a pick-up truck. David was driving and the other two were riding in the back. The paper said that the driver got out by rolling down the window and swimming to safety. The other two didn't make it – drowned 'cause they couldn't get the tailgate open.

Well, son, not much more news at this end; kind of quiet around here I sent your dad down to the post office to get stamps. He asked the lady how many 37-cent stamps he'd get if he bought a dozen. I tell you, son, this new math nowadays is more than we can handle.

Love,

Mom

XOXO

P.S. I was going to send some money but guess what – the envelope was already sealed.

Feel free to jot a personal note to whoever you may be sharing this book with. Better yet, tell them to go out and buy their own book.

SHAGGY DOG DITTY

Mahatma Gandhi, as you know, walked bare-foot most of the time, which produced an impressive set of calluses on his feet. He also ate very little, which made him rather frail and with his diet, he suffered from extremely bad breath.

This made him a what?

A super callused fragile mystic plagued with halitosis!

(Oh come on now, admit it, don't you just love it?)

* * * * * *

A young man was telling me that his father was a surgeon and that he was teasing his Dad just before sitting down to the family Thanksgiving dinner. "See how skillfully I carved the turkey, Dad. I'd make a pretty darn good surgeon, don't you think?" The father replied, "If you want to show me what a good surgeon you'd be, let's see you put it back together.

BEST BUMPER STICKERS

God Made Us Sisters; Prozac Made Us Friends

My Mother is a Travel Agent for Guilt Trips

Senior Citizens: Give Me My Damn Discount

I used to be Schizophrenic, But We're OK Now

Veni, Vedi, Visa: I Came, I Saw, I did a Little Shopping

What if the Hokey Pokey is Really What It's All About?

Coffee, Chocolate, Men; Some Things Are Just Better Rich.

Don't Treat Me Any Differently Than You Would the Queen

If You Want Breakfast in Bed, Sleep in the Kitchen

If at First You Don't Succeed, Skydiving Isn't For You

A Day without Sunshine is Like Night

First Things First, but Not Necessarily in That Order

Old Age Comes at a Bad Time

In America, Anyone Can Be President. That's One of the Risks You Take

All Men Are Idiots...and I Married Their King

The More You Complain, the Longer God Makes You Live

IRS: We've Got What It Takes to Take What You've Got

Hard Work Has a Future Payoff. Laziness Pays Off Now

As Long as there are Tests, There Will be Prayer in Public Schools

Hang Up and Drive

I Want to Die Peacefully in my Sleep Like My Grandfather...Not Screaming and Yelling Like the Passengers in his Car

I Took an IQ test and the Results Were Negative

Where there's a Will...I Want to be in it.

Consciousness: That annoying time between naps

Always Remember You're Unique...Just Like Everyone Else

Keep Honking While I Reload

Taxation WITH Representation Isn't So Hot Either!

Jack Kevorkian for White House Physician

My Wife Keeps Complaining I Never Listen to Her... or Something Like That

Sure, You Can Trust the Government! Just Ask an Indian!

* * * * * * *

Why is it that the older I get the longer it takes me to do things? Without going into all the details, I'll just tell you that lately it takes me two hours to watch 60 Minutes

* * * * * * *

This morning I woke up grumpy—next time I'm going to let her sleep.

DON'T GET PUSHY

A very wealthy man bought a huge ranch in Arizona and he invited some of his closest associates in to see it. After touring some of the 1500 acres of mountains and rivers and grasslands, he took everybody into the house. The house was as spectacular as the scenery, and out back was the largest swimming pool you have ever seen. However, this gigantic swimming pool was filled with alligators. The rich owner explained it this way: "I value courage more than anything else. Courage is what made me a billionaire. In fact, I think that courage is such a powerful virtue that if anybody is courageous enough to jump in that pool, swim through those alligators and make it to the other side, I'll give him anything he wants, anything – my house, my land, my money." Of course, everybody laughed at the absurd challenge and proceeded to follow the owner into the house for lunch...when they suddenly heard a splash. Turning around they saw this guy swimming for his life across the pool, thrashing at the water, as the alligators swarmed after him. After several death-defying seconds, the man made it, unharmed to the other side. The rich host was amazed, but he stuck to his promise. He said, "You are indeed a man of courage and I will stick to my word. What do you want? You can have anything – my house, my land, my money – just tell me what and it's yours." The swimmer, breathing heavily, looked up at his host and said, "I just want to know one thing, -- who pushed me into that pool?"

* * * * * * *

Let me share a true elderly-person-type story. It seems that this 87-year-old bachelor visited his doctor over at the Clinic. "Doctor, I've found a nice young lady that I want to marry!" Said the doctor, "Don't be silly! That could be fatal!" Said the old gent, "Well, so what? If she dies, she dies!"

* * * * * * *

The teacher asked, "Who was the first European to set foot in America?"

"Ohio," said one young student. "No, it was Columbus." "Yeah," replied the student, "so I forgot his first name."

A MAN OF FEW WORDS

An 80-year old man goes to a doctor for a check-up. The doctor tells him, "You are in terrific shape. There's nothing wrong with you. Why, you might live forever. By the way, how old was your father when he died?" The 80-year old patient responded, "Did I say he was dead?" The doctor couldn't believe it! So he said, "Well, how old was your grandfather when he died?" The 80-year old again responded, "Did I say he was dead?" The doctor was astonished. He said, "You mean to tell me you're 80 years old and both your father and grandfather are still alive?" "Not only that," said the patient, "my grandfather is 126 years old, and next week he's getting married for the first time!" The doctor said, "After 126 years of being a bachelor, why on earth did your grandfather want to get married?" His patient looked up at the doctor and said, "Did I say he wanted to."

* * * * * * *

Middle age is when broadness of the mind and narrowness of the waist change places.

TWO BITS OF NEWS

Bill went into his doctor's office to get the report on his recent physical examination. His doctor closed the office door and sat across from Bill. "The doctor said, "Bill, I'm afraid I have two bits of bad news." "Oh ya," said Bill. "What's the deal?" "Well Bill, first of all I'm afraid that you have terminal cancer." "Oh ya, what else?" "Bill, you also have Alzheimer's disease." Bill looked somewhat relived and said, "Thank goodness. I don't have cancer."

* * * * * * *

If you want to be happy for an hour, take a nap.

If you want to be happy for a day, go fishing.

If you want to be happy for a week, take a trip.

If you want to be happy for a year, inherit money.

If you want to be happy for a lifetime, serve others.

* * * * * * *

"THAT LOOK" KNOWS NO RESTRAINT

Three couples wanted to join the church. One couple was in their 60s, another in their 40s, and the newlywed couple in their 20s. The stern old pastor told them that there was just one more test to pass before they could become members. "Each of you must show self-discipline and inner strength—you may not have any physical contact with your spouse for one month; no hanky-panky whatsoever." In one month, the three couples returned to the pastor's office. The sixty-year-old couple reported, "No problem; it was easy." The forty-year-old couple said, "It was difficult but we made it." The newlyweds lowered their heads and said, "My wife gave me one of her special little smiles one day and...what more can I say; we couldn't abstain." The pastor looked at them sternly and said, "You are not welcome in this congregation." The young wife looked at him and replied, "Oh, great! We're not welcome at the Safeway market now either."

* * * * * * *

"OH NO"

It seems that a young German fella who was looking for work knocked at their door. "My name is Gunnar and I can do just about anything around de house and I verk very cheap." "How much would you charge to paint the porch out in front?" asked the woman. "Dat is easy verk; I do a good job for you for twenty dollars." "Excellent! Go ahead then," she instructed. "There's white paint in the garage." One half-hour later the fella knocked on the door again to say he was done. "Why, that didn't take you any time at all!" the woman remarked. Gunnar smiled, "Ya, looks real nice. But you ver mistaken about one thing—it vasn't a porch, it was a Mercedes."

* * * * * * *

While I was waiting for the elevator after visiting an old friend at the nursing home, I couldn't escape the conversation between a man and a lady resident. The man said, "Elizabeth, why don't you and I get married?" She answered, "Don't be silly, John! Who'd have us?"

HOW OLD DO YOU THINK I AM?

One sunny day in Pinetop, old Bill was taking a stroll down the hall at the local nursing home. As he passed by Martha's room, he stuck his head in the door and asked, "Martha, how old do you think I am?" Martha replied, "Go on with you, Bill. I'm watching my TV programs – don't bother me." On down the hall Bill shuffled until he got to Betty's room. He opened her door and said, "Betty, how old do you think I am?" Betty said, "Get out of here Bill. Can't you see I'm reading?" So, down the hall he went to Dorothy's door. Sticking his head in her room, he saw Dorothy just sitting looking out of the window. Again, Bill asked, "Dorothy, how old do you think I am?" Dorothy said, "Come in here Bill and stand here in front of me where I can see you." Bill did as Dorothy said and restated his question. "How old do you think I am?" The old gal looked up at him and said, "Drop your pants, Bill, shorts too." There he was standing in front of Dorothy with his pants and underpants down around his ankles. She said, "Now, turn around real slow." Bill did as he was told and when he had done a full 360 degrees, Dorothy said, "Bill, you're 92 years old." With amazement Bill said, "That's exactly right. How did you know?" Dorothy replied, "You told me yesterday, you damn fool."

* * * * * * *

After seeing the same patient for several nights, complaining of the same cold symptoms, the emergency physician finally gave in to his frustration. He had tried several different antibiotics and virtually every cold preparation he knew. He finally told the patient to go home and take four Ex-lax tablets and a glass of prune juice. "It won't do much for your cold symptoms, but it sure as heck will make you afraid to cough!"

* * * * * *

For all my golfing buddies, my next book is going to be titled "How To Line Up Your Fifth Putt."

* * * * * *

IS THIS JUST A BARNYARD FABLE?

Does this little story sound familiar?

Once upon a time, there was a little red hen that scratched about and uncovered some grains of wheat. She called her neighbors and said, "If we plant this wheat, we will all have bread to eat. Who will help me plant it?"

"Not I," said the cow. "Not I," said the duck. "Not I," said the goose. "Then I will," said the little red hen, and she did. The wheat grew tall and ripened into golden grain.

"Who will help me reap my wheat," asked the little red hen. "Not I," said the duck. "Out of my classification," said the pig. "I'd lose my seniority," said the cow. "I'd lose my unemployment insurance," said the goose. "Then I will," said the little red hen and she did.

At last, it came time to bake the bread. "That's overtime for me," said the cow. "I'm a dropout and never learned how," said the duck. "I'd lose my welfare payments," said the pig. "If I'm the only helper, that's discrimination," said the goose.

"Then I will," said the little red hen. She baked five loaves and held them up for her neighbors to see. They all wanted some and demanded a share. "No," said the little red hen, "I can eat the five loaves myself." "Excess profits!" carried the cow. "Capitalist leech!" screamed the duck. "Equal rights!" yelled the goose. They painted unfair picket signs and marched around the little red hen shouting obscenities.

The government agent came and said to the little red hen, "You must not be greedy. This is how our free enterprise system works. The productive workers must divide their products and wealth with the idle." And they all lived happily ever after. The little red hen smiled and clucked, "I'm grateful for what I have."

But her neighbors wondered why she never baked any more bread.

* * * * * * *

TELL IT LIKE IT IS

A California newspaper ran a classic story about the death of a woman's dog. When her beautiful dog died suddenly, the woman wanted to break the news gently to her five-year-old daughter. "We can all be happy now," she said, "that Frisky's up in heaven with God." Her daughter replied patiently,"Mom! What's God going to do with a dead dog?"

YES, FATHER, I CAN HEAR YOU SNORING

We moved my mother-in-law from Madison, WI to Oconomowoc, near to where we lived. We were lucky enough to get a beautiful, bright apartment on the third floor of Wilkinson Woods. Her living room looked out over the high school athletic field and tennis courts. She enjoyed hearing the band practice, the Friday night football games, and just the everyday comings and goings of the young people. The sunsets from her corner den were spectacular; overall, it was a very special location for Grandma.

However, there was one not-so-pleasant experience. In fact, snoring coming from the adjoining apartment kept her awake for several hours most every night. "Who is that snorting bull who lives on the other side of the bedroom wall?" Certainly, no average run-of-the-mill snorer could be heard through those well-insulated walls. This guy must be an Olympic, gold-medal snorer! After several discreet inquiries, it was learned that one of Grandma's very favorite people in all the world was the snore-king. To her surprise she found her neighbor was none other than Father Andre', the retired priest. All the residents- - no matter what religion, loved him. The good Father said Mass every Saturday evening in the first floor reception area. The elderly residents enjoyed his sermons and were quite thankful for receiving Communion each week. Father Andre' was indeed greatly appreciated in his retirement years but not appreciated at all for his "moonlight serenades."

Well. . . one Saturday after Mass had been completed and the residents were heading back to their apartments, Grandma found herself on the elevator with Father Andre'. After several people got off on the second floor, Father and Grandma were alone. After exchanging some general pleasantries, the Father said, "I understand that you are my next-door neighbor, is that true?"

Being assured that his information was correct, he said, "Would you mind if I asked you a personal question?"

Grandma thought for just a moment and said, "No, I don't mind." "Well," said the elderly priest, "Can you hear me snoring through the wall at night?"

Grandma took longer to answer this question. She surely didn't want to offend him or hurt his feelings but, on the other hand, he had asked her a direct question, and she didn't want to lie to him and, by golly, his loud snoring had been an unpleasant distraction for quite some time.

"Yes, I can hear you snoring, Father, and it's very loud."

He broke into a relieved, somewhat knowing, smile and said, "Good, I can hear you snoring also, and you too are very loud."

What's the old saying - - "It takes one to know one."

* * * * * * *

"Who is it?" asked St. Peter when he heard a knock at the Pearly Gates. "It is I," a voice answered. "Ah," smiled St. Peter, "another schoolteacher!"

* * * * * * *

SIGNS IN THE WINDOW

In a Rome Laundry:
"Ladies, leave your clothes here and spend the afternoon having a good time."

In an Acapulco hotel:
"The manager has personally passed all the water served here."

In Vet's Office:
"All unattended children will be given a free kitten."

Parking Lot outside Vet's Office:
"Parking for customers only, others will be neutered."

In Vet's Waiting Room:
"Be back in five minutes, Sit! Stay!"

Plumber:
"We repair what your husband fixed."

At a Tire Shop In Milwaukee:
"Invite us to your next blowout."

Door of Plastic Surgeon:
"Hello, we can help pick your nose."

At a Towing Company:
"We don't charge an arm and a leg. We want tows."

On an Electrician's Truck:
"Let us remove your shorts"

On a Maternity Room Door:
"Push, Push, Push."

At an Optometrists Office:
"If you don't see what you're looking for you've come to the right place."

In a Podiatrist's Office:
"Time wounds all heels."

Outside a Muffler Shop:
"No appointment necessary, we'll hear you coming."

In the Front Yard of a Funeral Home:
"Drive Carefully, We'll wait."

In a Counselors Office:
"Growing old is mandatory, growing wise is optional."

In a Radiator Repair Shop:
"It's a great place to take a leak."

* * * * * * *

Lay It On the Line - - Kids Do

Of all the subject matter a person has to write about, I think without a doubt the most fun things for me are the stories about kids and what comes out of their mouths. Every time I run across a cute and brutally honest "kids quote", I clip it or jot it down. Here is a recent collection to tickle your funny bone:

- Six-year-old Jim asked his Mom as she was tucking him in, "Are God and Santa Claus neighbors?"

- A young mother had just given birth to her fifth baby. One hectic morning the newest addition to the family was screaming, the mother's stitches were still hurting, and her sever-year-old reminded her that "Today is the Mother's Tea at school." Mom told her with a sigh, "I can't possibly go to the tea today, honey." The seven-year-old put her hands on her hips and admonished, "If you can't be there for ME, why are you still having more children?" Mom bundled up the newborn, squeezed into a dress and off they went to school.

- A five-year-old was talking about "bad words" with his dad. "Dad, do you know what is not nice to say?" The dad wondered what his young son was going to say. "Okay, what?" The boy whispered, "Son in a ditch."

- Unexpectedly during church, a four-year-old asked his parents when God was going to show up. "Son, God is invisible." The boy watched as the priest and altar boys and choir entered the sanctuary. Again, the boy asked in a loud voice, "God isn't with them; is He late?" Before his Mom could quiet him down, her son said quite firmly, "If he doesn't show up in 5 minutes, could we please leave?"

- Years ago, one of our sons was invited over to the youth minister's house for a special Sunday dinner. The pastor asked if Danny liked Sunday School. With total frustration, Dan said, "No. All we do is sit on our butts and color."

- A friend of mine and his wife retired upstairs for a little romance. When a neighbor lady knocked on the door and asked the youngest son where his Mommy and Daddy were, the boy replied, 'They're upstairs moving the furniture again."

- A rather precocious six-year-old with a real temper stomped up to her room and called down, "How do you spell hate?" Her mother called the answer up to her. Two minutes later the girl yelled again, "How do you spell love?" and the mother answered. Soon a note came fluttering down the stairs. "I hate you. Love, Mary."

- At dinner one night, our 16-year-old said that his assignment that day was to describe his father in one word. His Mom said, "Well, Doug, now that you are 16, describe yourself in one word." "Without hesitation he yelled, "Horny."

- The family was riding in the car one night and there was a fantastic crescent moon. Young Tom asked from the back seat, "Now, I wonder why God didn't turn that moon all the way on?"

* * * * * *

In a fourth grade classroom, the teacher had the kids telling about their ancestors. It was all she could do to keep from laughing when one young student said, "I can trace most of my ancestors back to Columbus. The rest go back to Toledo."

* * * * * *

AT-A-BOY DAD

A father and his small son were out walking one afternoon when the youngster asked how the electricity went through the wires stretched between the telephone poles. "Don't know," said the father. "Never knew much about electricity." A few blocks further the boy asked what caused lightning and thunder. "To tell the truth," said the father, "I never exactly understood that myself." The boy continued to ask questions throughout their walk, none of which the father could explain. Finally, as they were nearing home, the boy asked, "Pop, I hope you don't mind my asking so many questions. "Of course not," replied the father. "How else are you going to learn?"

* * * * * * *

You know you're getting old when you start dispensing the advice you never followed as a youth.

GOTCHA

A golfer is in a competitive match with a friend, who is ahead by a couple of strokes. The golfer says to himself, "I'd give anything to sink this next putt." A stranger walks up to him and whispers, "Would you give up a fourth of your sex life?" The golfer thinks the man is crazy and that his answer will be meaningless. At the same time, he thinks this might be a good omen, so he says, "Okay." And sinks the putt. Two holes later, he mumbles to himself, "Boy, if I could only get an eagle on this hole." The same stranger moves to his side and says, "Would it be worth another fourth of your sex life?" The golfer shrugs and says, "Sure," and he makes an eagle. On the final hole, the golfer needs yet another eagle to win. Though he says nothing the stranger moves to his side and says. "Would you be willing to give up the rest of your sex life to win this match?" The golfer says, "Certainly!" Again, he makes an eagle. As the golfer walks to the clubhouse, the stranger walks alongside and says, "You know, I've really not been fair with you because you don't know who I am. I'm the devil, and from now on you will have no sex life." "Nice to meet you," says the golfer, "I'm Father O'Malley."

* * * * * * *

BENEFITS OF GROWING OLDER

- People call at 8 p.m. and say, "Did I wake you?"

- Things you buy now won't wear out.

- You can eat dinner at 4:00 p.m.

- You can't remember the last time you lay on the floor to watch television.

- You have a party and the neighbors don't even realize it.

- You quit trying to hold your stomach in, no matter who walks into the room

- You send money to PBS

- You sing along with the elevator music.

- Your ears are hairier than your head.

- Your eyes won't get much worse.

- Your joints are more accurate than the National Weather Service

- Your secrets are safe with your friends because they can't remember them either.

- Your supply of brain cells is finally down to a manageable size.

* * * * * * *

IT'S THE LITTLE THINGS IN LIFE
THAT COUNT

All too often, we think that it's the big, spectacular, and expensive things that we say and do that are lasting and important. Wrong. Before I tell you my story, I'm, reminded of something Helen Keller said: "I am only one; but still I am one. I cannot do everything, but still I can do something; I will not refuse to do the something I can do." You see, it's the small, everyday things that each of us can do that makes every one of us true ministers.

Harry never even vaguely considered himself a minister in his church or in his community. "Come on," he would say. "The people who preach and give out the wine and bread at communion and read the Scriptures, they are the ministers, but me . . . I'm just an usher."

A young pastor in Harry's church had given a talk on the "ministry" of being a greeter and an usher, but Harry wasn't buying that "malarkey". He said that he was just trying to "give the real pastors a hand" by taking the collection, steering people to the altar at Holy Communion, and saying "Hello" to fellow parishioners when they came into church.

Harry believed all of this until one cold wintry night when he came home from work and his wife told him the pastor had called. Harry returned the call and the pastor told him that a letter had been received at the church office. The letter was simply addressed to "Harry The Usher".

The pastor said that since he was the only usher called Harry, would he please drop by and pick up his letter. Harry, intrigued by the request, stopped at the church on his way home the next day, ripped open the envelope and in the dim light of the car, read the following:

Dear Harry,

I don't know your last name, but I guess that's fair. You don't know mine either. I'm Gert, Gert from the 10:30 service. I'm writing you for a couple of reasons, and I hope you will understand.

One of the reasons is to ask a favor. I am not particularly close to any of the pastors at church but somehow I feel close to you. I don't even know how you got to know my first name, but every Sunday morning when I walked into church, you smiled and greeted me by my name. We would exchange a few words that were perhaps meaningless to most – like how bad the weather was, how much you liked my Sunday hat or how late I was on a particular Sunday.

I don't have any close family left, Harry. My husband has been dead for 16 years now and the kids are scattered. Not too many people smile and greet an old lady like me, but you did.

Harry, in the little time left to me, I just wanted to say thank you. Thank you for your thoughtfulness, for remembering my name is Gert, for the smiles and the little laughter, the consideration and the conversation.

Now for the favor. I am dying, Harry. My time is running out. It is not important that you come to my wake, but what is important to me is that when they bring me to church for services for the last time, you will be standing at the front entrance. It just wouldn't seem right if you weren't standing there to say, "Hello, Gert. Good to see you."

If you are there, Harry, I will feel assured that your warm hospitality in my home church will be duplicated by Jesus in my new home. I hope people in heaven will say as you always did. "Hello, Gert. It is good to see you."

With love and gratitude,

Gert

A short time later Gert was buried. Harry did stand at the church entrance. He smiled and said the words Gert wanted to hear as he gently touched her coffin. He found out at that moment that it wasn't "malarkey". Harry had become a true minister.

* * * * * *

GOD ONLY KNOWS

A young man once asked God how long a million years was to Him.

God replied, "A million years to me is just like a single second in your time."

Then the young man asked God what a million dollars was to Him.

God replied, "A million dollars to me is just like a single penny to you."

Then the young man got his courage up and asked:"God, could I have one of your pennies?

God smiled and replied, "Certainly, just a second."

* * * * * *

"I'LL HAVE A DOUBLE DIP CHOCOLATE CONE, PLEASE"

Sometimes when you least expect them, opportunities present themselves and events turn out to be priceless events. If we can just remember to keep our eyes and ears open, there are wonderful human things going on all around us. I have to tell you of one such happening—this was a once-in-a-lifetime experience.

It was a hot sticky afternoon, and I was driving north of Pinetop. One of those hot summer days when playing hooky could happen without much guilt - - maybe none. I was about ready for a tall, cold lemonade when I spotted a drugstore on Main Street. Perfect. I pulled up into the parking space next to the curb. Sitting on the curb in front of the drugstore were three small kids. Two of the little urchins were rag-tag-looking five-year-old boys and between them was their "victim" - - a cute little four or five-year-old girl, all with skinned knees. The three of them were perfect for a Norman Rockwell, small-town summertime painting.

I stayed in the car with the windows down and listened as the two boys told the little gal, "If you take this gum wrapper into the drugstore and give it to the man, he'll give you a double-dip ice cream cone- - for free." (The gum wrapper was all torn and dirty.) I quickly got out of the car and hurried into the drugstore. I told the young man behind the soda fountain that, when the little girl in the blue dress came in, to give her a double-dip cone—whatever flavor she wanted—and I gave him a couple of dollars.

Well, the cute little thing walked in, stretched to her fullest to put the gum wrapper up on the counter and said, "I would like a double-dip chocolate cone, please." The two dirty-nosed boys, with their faces pressed against the front window, were in stitches. They had really put one over on their little friend, and they were enjoying every minute of it.

Expressions changed quite rapidly, however, when they saw the man hand the girl an extra-large double-dip chocolate cone. Their expressions as the small girl walked out the door and down the street were priceless. The two boys nearly knocked each other over getting back to the curb to look for dirty, torn gum wrappers. Best money I ever spent.

* * * * * * *

WORDS GET ALL 'KITTYWAMPUS' IN THE TRANSLATION

Whether you realize it or not, we all use tools in just about everything we do. The tools of an artist are his paint, brushes and canvas. A carpenter uses hammer, saw and nails, and to a writer words are his tools. I think you'll all agree that sometimes language and the way that words are used is truly a laughing matter. I have to thank Maggie, an old girlfriend of mine for sharing the following communications gems.

It all starts in various foreign countries where applying the grammar of one language to the spoken and written works of another can produce some very humorous translations:

Sign in a Tokyo hotel: "Is forbidden to steal hotel towels please. If you are not person to do such thing, please not to read notice."

In a Bucharest hotel lobby: "The lift is being fixed for the next day. During that time, we regret that you will be unbearable.

In a Belgrade hotel elevator: To move the cabin, push button for wishing floor. If the cabin should enter more persons, each one should press a number of wishing floor. Driving is then going alphabetically by national order."

In a Paris hotel elevator: "Please leave your values at the front desk."

In a Japanese hotel: "You are invited to take advantage of the chambermaid."

In an Austrian hotel catering to skiers: "Not to perambulate the corridors in the hours of repose in the boots of ascension."

On the menu of a Swiss restaurant: "Our wines leave you nothing to hope for."

<u>Outside a Paris dress shop</u>: "Dresses for street walking."

<u>In a Zurich hotel</u>: "Because of the impropriety of entertaining guests of the opposite sex in the bedroom it is suggested that the lobby be used for this purpose."

<u>In an advertisement by a Hong Kong dentist</u>: "Teeth extracted by the latest Methodists."

<u>In a Rome laundry</u>: "Ladies, leave your clothes here and spend the afternoon having a good time."

<u>In a Czechoslovakian tourist agency</u>: "Take one of our horse-driven city tours—we guarantee no miscarriages."

<u>Outside a Hong Kong tailor shop</u>: "Ladies may have a fit upstairs."

<u>A sign posted in Germany's Black Forest</u>: "It is strictly forbidden on our black forest camping site that people of different sex. For instance, men and women, live together in one tent unless they are married with each other for that purpose."

<u>In a Copenhagen airline ticket office</u>: "We take your bags and send them in all directions."

<u>In a Norwegian cocktail lounge</u>: "Ladies are requested not to have children in the bar."

In the office of a Roman doctor: "Specialist in women and other diseases."

From a Japanese information booklet about using a hotel air conditioner: "Colles and Heates: If you want just condition of warm in your room, please control yourself."

From a brochure of a car rental firm in Tokyo: "When passenger of foot are in sight, tootie the horn. Trumpet him melodiously at first, but if he still obstacles your passage then tootie him with vigor."

* * * * * * *

SIX MONTHS A CATHOLIC

We live in Green Valley, AZ (just south of Tucson) for six months of winter and in Pinetop, AZ for six months during the summer. Best of both worlds.

While in Green Valley, we belong to the Lutheran Church. After visiting several churches in Pinetop, we fell in love with a dear sweet Father at the Catholic Church. He was born and raised in Ireland and still has that thick and beautiful Irish brogue that you could cut with a knife, and a sense of humor to go along with it.

One Sunday before Mass started, the good Father came up to me and said, "David me boy, I have a new concept of what Hell is like." I replied, "Oh, do you? Tell me what Hell is like." He went on, "Hell is not hot, no fire at all. In fact, Hell is 60° below zero all the time." I said, "Well, IF any of us Lutherans ever go to Hell, I suppose all we'll have to wear is a light weight sweater for the 60° below." The good Father said, "No David, all you Lutherans will be naked." Amen!

* * * * * *

READY FOR A PARTY

Sam has been a wildlife biologist studying shrew behavior for 25 years and is finally ready to sit down and write his doctoral dissertation. He finds the perfect writing spot, 50 acres of land in the Tennessee mountains as far from humanity as possible. Sam sees the postman once a week and gets groceries once a month. Otherwise, it's total peace and quiet. After six months or so of almost total isolation, he's finishing dinner when someone knocks on his door. He opens it and there is a big, bearded man standing there. "Name's Bo...your neighbor from four miles away...Having a party Saturday...thought you'd like to come." "Great," says Sam, "after six months out here I'm ready to meet some local folks. Thank you." As Bo is leaving he stops, "Gotta warn you there's gonna be some drinkin'.'' "Not a problem...after 25 years in the wildlife business, I can drink with the best of 'em." Again, as he starts to leave Bo stops. "More 'n' likely gonna be some fightin' too." Sam says, "Well, I get along with people. I'll be there. Thanks again." Once again, Bo turns from the door. "I've seen some wild sex at these parties, too." "Now that's not a problem" says Sam, "I've been all alone for six months! I'll definitely be there...by the way, what should I wear?" Bo stops in the door again and says, "Whatever you want, it's just gonna be the two of us."

* * * * * * *

After going to their local bank to get a loan to buy a larger house, a young couple told their six-year-old that they had to move because another baby was coming. "Aw, that won't work," frowned the youngster, "He'll just follow us."

* * * * * * *

A friend of mine in Detroit who had gone about six miles in a taxi when he discovered that he had left his wallet at home and had no cash for the fare. Knowing he was in trouble, he said to the taxi driver, "Stop at this hardware store and wait. I need to go in and buy a flashlight so I can look for the hundred dollar bill I dropped back here." When he came out of the store, the taxi was gone.

* * * * * *

OUT OF THE MOUTHS OF BABES

To me, there is no purer humor than the real-life, everyday, honest responses that young people come out with. Let's look at some of the questions and answers that are heard in Sunday school? It doesn't really matter what church you go to---kids are kids.

When asked "Who was Noah's wife?" the answer came back: "Joan of Ark."

A fourth grade class was in the process of memorizing the Ten Commandments. Billy recited the fourth commandment: "Humor thy father and thy mother."

On an exam given to a high school class one Sunday, the instruction was "Write what you know about Lot's wife." The teacher was surprised to read one of the answers. "Lot's wife was a pillar of salt by day but a ball of fire at night."

One Sunday morning the kids were talking about marriage. Tammy was certain that "holy acrimony" was another name for marriage. The teacher was able to keep a straight face until little

Scott stood up and shared his knowledge: "Christians can have only one wife; this is called monotony."

Bonnie did a research paper on the Pope. She started her report by saying, "The Pope lives in a vacuum." You'll also be glad to know that Sheri did a paper on cherubims and seraphims, and she says that the next angels in line are the paraffins.

I love the answer that Patrick gave to a very complicated question. "Abraham begat Isaac and Isaac begat Jacob and Jacob begat twelve partridges." Debbie was explaining to her class why Protestants are luckier than Catholics: "Because when we die, we don't have to go through a percolator to get to heaven."

Here is one that doubled me over. One blistering hot day last summer, with guests present for dinner, little Tommy's mother asked him to say the blessing. "But, Mom," the boy protested, "I don't know what to say." "Just say what you've heard me say," she advised. So Tommy obediently bowed his head and prayed, "Dear Lord, please explain to me why in the world I invited all these people here on a hot day like this."

The second grade teacher said to David, "I'll ask you a question and you answer. Then you ask me a question and I'll answer." The teacher asked, "Why do children get dirtier than adults?"

David's answer, "Cause they're closer to the ground." Now it was David's turn to ask the question. "How deep would the ocean be if there weren't any sponges?" The teacher's response, "From now on, I'll ask the questions."

* * * * * * *

AIN'T IT THE TRUTH

Before you criticize someone, walk a mile in his shoes. That way, if he gets angry, he'll be a mile away – and barefoot.

A clear conscience is usually the sign of a bad memory.

My idea of housework is to sweep the room with a glance.

I have found that at my age going bra-less pulls all the wrinkles out of my face.

For every action, there is an equal and opposite government program.

Age is a very high price to pay for maturity.

A closed mouth gathers no feet.

* * * * * * *

A father is someone who carries pictures where his money used to be.

* * * * * *

Think about it: "Always forgive your enemies—
nothing annoys them so much."

* * * * * *

DEAR GRANDMA

"Those good times shared in past Decembers,
the mind still sees, the heart remembers."
There seems to be a special, almost magical
experience and relationship that happens between young children and their grandparents.
For those of us who remember our grandparents, or for those who are now in the grandpar-
ent category, or for those young parents who
can see this magic between their kids and their
parents—whatever your situation, I thought
you'd get a kick out of a letter a third grader
wrote to her grandma telling her what a
grandma is:

Dear Grandma,

A grandmother is a lady who has no children of
her own so she likes other people's little girls.
A grandfather is a man grandmother. He goes
for walks with the boys and they talk about
fishing and tractors and like that.

Grandmas don't have to do anything except be there. They are old, so they shouldn't play hard or run. It is enough if they drive us to the market where the pretend horse is and have lots of dimes ready for us. Or if they take us for walks, they should slow down past things like pretty leaves or caterpillars. They should never say, "Hurry up."

Usually they are fat, but not too fat to tie kids' shoes. They wear glasses and funny underwear. They can take their teeth and gums off.

It is better if they don't typewrite, or play Old Maid except with us. They don't have to be smart, only answer questions like why dogs hate cats, and how come God isn't married. They don't talk baby talk like visitors do because it is hard to understand. When they read to us, they don't skip or mind if it is the same story again.

Everybody should try to have one, especially if they don't have television, because grandmas are the only grownups who have got time.

* * * * * * *

READY FOR ANOTHER BLONDE JOKE

Two blondes were hiking in the forest—along a river. Without realizing it, they became separated--one blonde on one side of the river and the other on the far side. The one yelled across to the other one, "How can I get to the other side?" The other yelled back, "Honey, you are on the other side."

THE MAMMOGRAM

This is an X-ray that has its own name because no one wants to actually say the word *breast.*

Mammograms require your *breast* to do gymnastics. If you have extremely agile *breasts,* you should do fine. Most *breasts*, however, pretty much hang around doing nothing in particular, so they are woefully unprepared.

BUT you can prepare for a mammogram right at home using these simple exercises.

EXERCISE 1: Refrigerate two bookends overnight. Lay one of your breasts (Either will do) between the two bookends and smash the bookends together as hard as you can. Repeat three times daily.

EXERCISE 2: Locate a pasta maker or old wringer washer. Feed the breasts into the machine and start cranking. Repeat twice daily.

EXERCISE 3: (Advanced) Situate yourself comfortably on your side on the garage floor. Place one of your breasts snugly behind the rear tire of the family van. When you give the signal, hubby will slowly ease the car into re-verse. Hold for five seconds. Repeat on the other side.

* * * * * * *

THIS IS A TEST

Each question contains the initials of words that will make it correct. Your job is to come up with the missing words. Let me get you started. Here's a freebie. 26 – L of the A (The answer is 26 Letters of the Alphabet.)

1. 7 - D of the W
2. 12 - S of the Z
3. 1001 - A N
4. 54 - C in a D (w/js)
5. 9 - P in the S S
6. 88 - K on a P
7. 13 - S on the A F
8. 32 - D F at which W F
9. 18 - H on a G C
10. 90 - D in a R A
11. 8 - S on a S S
12. 3 - B M (S H T R)
13. 4 - Q in a G
14. 24 - H in a D

15. I - W on a U
16. 5 - d in a Z C ~
17. 57 - H V
18. 11 - P on a FB T
19. 1000 - W that a P is W ~
20. 29 - D in F in a L Y
21. 64 - S on a C B
22. 40 - D and N of the G F ~
23. 76 - T in the B P
24. 50 - W to L Y L ~
25. 99 - B of B on the W ~
26. 9 - J on the S C ~
27. 7 - B for S B
28. 21 - D on a D ~
29. 1- H on a U ~
30. 60 - S in a M
31. 200 - D to P G in M

There now. Wasn't that challenging? It's all right that you didn't get them all right away. Maybe you didn't get them all, even with help from your better half. I figure that on this test, I wouldn't give you the answers right away. You probably would like to think on some of them for a while. I'll give you the correct answers at the end of the book. As my wife said, "Oh, I just hate when you do that."

* * * * * * *

"TRIED IT ONCE"

A business acquaintance was in London on a foggy night, and he went to a private club where he had a guest membership. Hoping to strike up a conversation with a distinguished-looking Englishman sitting nearby, he said, "May I buy you a drink?" "No," said the Britisher coolly. "Don't drink. Tried it once and I didn't like it." After my friend ordered a drink, he tried to make conversation again. "Would you like a cigar?" "No. Don't smoke. Tried tobacco once and I didn't like it." My friend thought for a minute and then said, "Would you like to join me in a game of gin rummy?" "No. Don't like card games. Tried it once and I didn't like it. However, my son will be dropping in after a bit. Perhaps he will join you." My friend settled back in his chair and said, "Your only son, I presume?"

* * * * * * *

A doctor came home from a hard day at the hospital only to find his basement flooded. He called a plumber, who fixed the problem in five minutes, then presented a bill for $200.00. "That's outrageous!" the doctor bellowed. "I'm a surgeon and even I don't make that kind of money!" "Neither did I when I was a surgeon," said the plumber.

A WEEK UP NORTH WITH THE BOYS

Not long ago, my wife and I had a chance to get together with some old high school and college friends. Half the fun of seeing old classmates every ten years or so is to rehash memories and to see which of them has gained more weight and gotten older looking than you.

I'll share one of my favorites from that wonderful summer of 1950. At the time, it wasn't at all funny, but looking back, I have to chuckle—every time I think of our first attempt at a beer party.

Bill's parents had a cottage in northern Wisconsin. Six of us--all fifteen years old—decided we'd spend a week up at the cottage—away from parents and girls. Girls you didn't know were always better when you're on vacation. My folks volunteered to drive us up to the cabin, drop us off, and go on their way for a little vacation of their own. None of us had a driver's license—one year away from being real men. We made it to Turtle Lake in what seemed to be fifty hours. You see, my Mom kept encouraging us to sing what she called "the good old songs." Oh, brother. "Mom, the guys don't feel like singing all the way to Turtle Lake." "Okay, then we'll play 20 questions."

We pulled in the drive and unloaded the car as fast as we could. The guys thanked my folks and I kissed Mother dear goodbye. We all waved as their car disappeared down the tree-lined dirt road. Free at last! One solid week of telling dirty jokes, fishing, smoking cigars, eating beans and wieners, checking out the local babes, playing cards, and yes siree, drinking beer.

Bill's folks had an old pier and an even older wooden rowboat. Not to worry—we'll row across the lake, buy five or six six-packs of cheap local brew for starters, and let the fun begin. We made it to the general store across the lake in record time, bought the beer and some minor incidentals like bread, eggs and a quart of milk—didn't want to waste our money on junk food. Ned was elected to go in and buy the beer because he had started shaving that summer—he looked older.

As we were rowing back to the cabin, about halfway across the lake, one of the guys said, "Cazzy, isn't that your mom and Dad standing on the pier?" Oh Lord, have mercy—it was them. They had forgotten to give us something and before driving too far, had turned around and come back to the cabin. Panic time for the party animals. What do we do with all this valuable beer? Tom had a cool head. "Just act calm. Put the six packs in this big fish net, and I'll tie a rope around it and lower the whole thing slowly into the lake. They'll never see it." As we got closer, but not too close, I hollered,

"Hi, Mom and Dad. What do you want?" They said they had forgotten to leave one of the boys his allergy pills. "We'll just leave the bottle of pills on the porch and be on our way. We love you kids." Mom, PLEASE! Being 40 yards off shore and with the beer 40 feet underwater, we were safe. No one's the wiser. "Okay, they're gone. Get the beer back in the boat and let's get on with party time." The look on Tom's face told the whole story. Yup, the rope had broken and our six packs were at the bottom of Turtle Lake. No beer, not $25.00 between us, and a week to go. We tried to talk Tom into learning how to deep-sea dive, but he didn't like that idea. We tried dragging the bottom of the lake with every lure in our tackle boxes, but all we got were some northerns, some bass, few good-sized walleyes—not a successful week at all.

Years later my Mom asked one day, "Did you boys ever get that beer off the bottom of Turtle Lake?" And to think we thought all parents were slow. NO WAY!

* * * * * * *

WHY

Why do they put Braille dots on the keypad of the drive-up ATM?

Why is it that when you transport something by car, it's called a shipment, but when you transport something by ship, its called cargo?

Why is it that when you're driving and looking for an address, you turn down the volume on the radio?

Why isn't phonetic spelled the way it sounds?

How does the guy who drives the snowplow get to work in the mornings?

If a cow laughed, would milk come out of her nose?

If nothing ever sticks to TEFLON, how do they make TEFLON stick to the pan?

* * * * * * *

QUIRKY ONE LINERS

Never raise your hands to your kids. It leaves you groin unprotected.

I'm not into working out. My philosophy is no pain, no pain.

I'm in shape. Round is a shape.

I'm desperately trying to figure out why Kamikaze pilots wore helmets.

I've always wanted to be somebody, but I should have been more specific.

Ever notice when you blow in a dog's face he gets mad at you, but when you take him in a car he sticks his head out the window?

Ever notice that anyone going slower than you is an idiot, but anyone going faster than you is a maniac?

You have to stay in shape. My mother started walking five miles a day when she was 60. She's 90 now and we have no idea where she is.

I have six locks on my door, all in a row. When I go out, I lock every other one. I figure no matter how long somebody stands there picking the locks; they are always locking three of them.

One out of every three Americans is suffering from some form of mental illness. Think of two of your best friends. If they are OK, then it must be you.

Ask people why they have deer heads on their walls and they will tell you it's because they're such beautiful animals. I think my wife is beautiful, but I only have photographs of her on the wall.

Future historians will be able to study at the Jimmy Carter Library, the Gerald Ford Library, the Ronald Reagan Library, and the Bill Clinton Adult Bookstore.

At the cocktail party, one woman said to another, "Aren't you wearing your wedding ring on the wrong finger?" The other replied, "Yes, I am – I married the wrong man."

The groom, upon his engagement, went to his father and said, "I've found a woman just like mother!" His father replied, "So what do you want from me, sympathy?"

If you want your spouse to listen and pay strict attention to every word you say, talk in your sleep.

I married Miss Right. I just didn't know her first name was Always.

A man rushes into his house and yells to his wife, "Martha, pack up your things! I just won the California lottery!" Martha replies, "Shall I pack for warm weather or cold?" The man responds, "I don't care, just so long as you're out of this house by noon!"

I haven't spoken to my wife in 18 months – I don't like to interrupt her.

Just think, if it weren't for marriage, men would go through life thinking they had no faults at all.

A couple was having a discussion about family finances. Finally, the husband exploded, "If it weren't for my money, this house wouldn't be here!" The wife, replied, "My dear, if it weren't for your money, I wouldn't be here!"

A man said his credit card was stolen but he decided not to report it because the thief was spending less than his wife did.

First guy (proudly): "My wife's an angel!" Second guy: "You're lucky, mine's still alive."

Women will never be equal to man until they can walk down the street with a bald head and a beer gut, and still think they are beautiful.

* * * * * * *

How about the story of the student who was writing a term paper on the United States/Japan trade situation. "Dad," asked the son, "what factors influence the balance of trade?" "Well," his father said thoughtfully, "there are changes in exchange rates, tariffs, cultural differences, savings versus consumption, competitive advantages, economic recessions, local government intervention . . . .

"Look, Dad," the boy interrupted, "if you don't know, just say so."

* * * * * * *

HEARING AIDS AND FALSE TEETH

Will someone please tell me why we feel we have to hide the fact that we use one, two, or all of the above? I can understand why there are those who want to keep their age or their weight a secret, but when parts of the old body start to show signs of wear, why be ashamed or afraid to admit it.

I admire people who wear hearing aids and don't feel they have to hide them. Losing your teeth for one reason or another? Get a good set of dentures, smile, eat sweet corn, and kiss your partner. Your arms ain't long enough anymore to hold the newspaper so you can read it. Get a pair of horn rims and start appreciating the world again.   I have trifocals and now can thread a needle, read the sports page, and watch the geese fly south (not all at the same time). When it comes to hiding the natural color of your hair or plopping a "rug" on top of your head, I don't agree with a lot of people. If I'm supposed to be gray or white or bald or kind of bald (called "thinning"), then so be it. I'll be damned if I'm going to lose sleep over the color or amount of hair on my head.

This brings me to a cute story about an amazing 75-year-old aunt of mine. Her name is Eliza but she's been known as Liz for as long as pickles have been green.

Liz and her husband Marz have always been involved up to their eyeglasses in worthwhile activities like Habitat for Humanity, feeding the homeless, repairing and replacing things for people who need help. If there were 28 hours in the day, Marz and Liz would be happily busy helping others.

Not long ago this twosome (75 years going on 45) was in one of the southern states helping to build a church. Liz spent the afternoon on the roof nailing down shingles. She said the sun was hot and her bones were letting her know it was about time to get back down to earth. After a nice hot shower, Liz fought to keep her eyes open during dinner. She couldn't wait to hit her cot in the local high school gym, the gals in one section and guys in the other.

As always, Liz put her false teeth in a big glass of water, washed her face and crashed for the night. The next morning she got up, retrieved her teeth, washed her face, and realized she didn't have her hearing aid in her ear. "Now where in the heck did I put that darn thing?" She looked under and around her makeshift bed. Others joined in the search for the missing earpiece, but it was nowhere to be found. All of a sudden, Liz realized what she had done. Yup, there was the hearing aid—in the glass of water where her teeth had been. They all had a good laugh and warned her not to get so tired that she'd make the same mistake again. The funniest part, though, was when Liz told me, "It took three whole days to dry the crazy thing out; sounded like I was under Niagara Falls."

I get a kick out of the message on their home answering machine. "We cannot take your call right now. We are up on the roof replacing shingles. If you will please leave your name and number, we'll get back to you just as soon as our neighbors bring back the ladder."

So, I guess the bottom line is to accept with humble dignity the inevitable and, above all, be thankful for what we have, and don't ever underestimate the power of a good sense of humor.

* * * * * * *

"Practice makes perfect, so be careful what you practice.

* * * * * * *

If you look like your passport picture, you probably need the trip.

HO HO HO – HERE COMES SANTA CLAUS

When Santa comes to your house, it's a very special time for everybody. He may stop at your place on Christmas Eve or sometime during the night – maybe on Christmas morning.

Whenever he comes to bring your presents, he also brings a child-like excitement that's hard to describe. The whole ritual of leaving a light on for him, some cookies and milk, and, for sure, something for his reindeer. That's all part of this very special and exciting time – no matter what your age.

Well, let me tell you about a truly memorable Christmas Eve and a Santa Claus experience that was certainly exciting in every sense of the word.

My boss, Bob, lived in a lovely, large home in a very nice section of town. He had four young children and a wonderful wife; his elderly mother lived with them. Shortly before Christmas, Bob said that he wished he knew of a good Santa Claus who could come to his house on Christmas Eve and hand out the presents to everybody. He wanted his kids and all the family to be able to see Santa and make the evening even more special and exciting.

I told Bob that my dad had a Santa Claus suit and had played Santa several times in the past. I thought that my father would make a perfect Santa and would be happy to be Santa for Bob and his family. Besides, if my dad did a great job and everything worked out well, it sure wouldn't hurt my job security, now would it? Anyway, all the details were arranged and the stage was set.

My dad took great pains to see that every detail was perfect. From the black boots, black belt, full snow-white beard, white trim all the way up the bright red suit, to the tip of his bright red hat – everything looked totally professional – he was Santa Claus. I drove him over to Bob's house and parked down the street so no one would see my car. I gave dad some final instructions: "The big cloth sack full of presents was on the front porch. Lots of HO HO Hos, lots of noise and commotion, and then they'll ask you to come in the house. The living room is off the foyer to the left. . . "The seven-foot flocked Christmas tree was decorated like a million dollars. The entire home was magnificent in every way.

I watched as Santa made his way up the long walkway to the house. Oh, yes, one detail I forgot to tell you – Santa couldn't see a thing without his glasses. I mean, not even his hand in front of his face. He did not have his glasses on because they didn't fit in with the costume. Big mistake No. 1.

I watched as Santa bumped into one of the large pillars by the front door – he almost tripped over the bag of presents – and none to soon was invited by Bob into the house. I could see the young ones running and jumping with excitement as Santa entered the living room. I saw Bob's elderly mother stand up, with some help, to greet Santa. Are you ready for this? I watched from the front lawn as Santa bumped full force and headlong into grandmother, knocking her boldly into the seven-foot flocked tree. Yup, the tree fell over with grandma spread-eagled in the middle of it, both on the floor. HO HO HO!

You talk about excitement and hustle and bustle. Let me tell you – Santa didn't take long to distribute the gifts. He helped get grandma out of the tree, back into her chair, a couple of HO HOs, and he was out of there. "Well, Dad, so much for my job security."

But, all is well that ends well. Bob and his wife assured us the next day that his mother came through the ordeal with only minor scratches; however, the Christmas tree was never quite the same. Funny thing. Bob never mentioned needing a Santa the next year.

* * * * * * *

OLD AGE AIN'T FOR SISSIES

On a Saturday in mid-September the whole family gathered for a very special 90th birthday party. There were sisters and brothers from California, aunts, uncles and cousins from all four corners, and grandchildren from who knows where. Yup, Mom turned 90.

When you get up in years, you can get away with saying and doing things that would be considered no-no's for a younger person. I remember an older friend who was honored at a gathering given for him. The place was a very swank club and the food was out of this world. They served an assortment of hors d' oeuvres that I had never tasted or heard of before. A fancy tray of beautifully prepared seafood delicacies was passed to the ninety-year-old guest of honor. "I'd like to know what this stuff costs 'cause it tastes like hell."

My dear sweet mother, who wouldn't say a harsh word to anyone, came out with an unexpected blast on her last trip to the emergency room at Madison General Hospital. As she lay in a semi-coma in the ER, we were gathered around her bedside expecting that this would be it. As we sat quietly holding her hands, they wheeled a youngster into the cubicle next to hers—the only thing separating the two beds was a cloth drape. The kid must have cut himself and the doc was stitching him up. You could hear the boy screaming five counties away. Out of her coma my soft-spoken, kindly old mama said, "Will someone please go over there and slap that little bastard."

Mom's ideas about being 90:

"I have good news for you. The first 90 years are the hardest. The second 90 are going to be a succession of parties.

Once you have passed 90, everyone wants to carry your baggage and help you up the steps. If you forget your name or anybody else's name, or an appointment, or your own telephone number, or promise to be at three places at the same time, or can't remember how many grandkids you have, you need only explain that you are 90.

If you survive until you are 90, everybody is surprised that you are still alive. They treat you with respect just for having lived so long. Another good thing about turning 90 is that I won't ever have to go to another high school class reunion."

* * * * * * *

LUTHERAN AIRLINES, INC.

If you are traveling soon, consider Lutheran Air, the no-frills airline. You're all in the same boat on Lutheran Air, where flying is an uplifting experience. There is no First Class on any Lutheran Air flight. Meals are potluck. Rows 1-6 bring rolls, 7-15 bring a salad, 16-21 a main dish, and 22-30 a dessert. Basses and tenors please sit in the rear of the aircraft. Everyone is responsible for his or her own baggage. All fares are by freewill offering and the plane will not land until the budget is met.

Pay attention to your flight attendant, who will acquaint you with the safety system aboard this Lutheran Air 599. Okay then, listen up: I'm only gonna say this once. In the event of a sudden loss of cabin pressure, I am frankly going to be real surprised and so will Captain Orson because we fly right around 2000 feet, so loss of cabin pressure would probably indicate the Second Coming or something of that nature, and I wouldn't bother with those little masks on the rubber tubes. You're gonna have bigger things to worry about than that. Just stuff those back up in their little holes. Probably the masks fell out because of turbulence which, to be honest with you, we're going to have quite a bit of at 2000 feet---sort of like driving across a plowed field, but after awhile you get used to it.

In the event of a water landing, I'd say forget it. Start saying the Lord's Prayer and just hope you get to the part about forgive us our sins as we forgive those who sin against us, which some people say "trespass against us" which isn't right, but what can you do?

The use of cell phones on the plane is strictly forbidden, not because they may interfere with the plane's navigational system, which is seat of the pants all the way—no, it's because cell phones are a pain in the wazoo and if God meant you to use a cell phone, He would have put your mouth on the side of your head.

We're going to start lunch right about noon and its buffet style with the coffee pot up front. Then we'll have the hymn sing---hymnals in the seat pocket in front of you. Don't take yours with you when you go or I am going to be real upset and I am not kidding! Right now I'll say Grace—God is Great and God is good and we thank Him for the food, Father, Son and Holy Ghost. May we land in Tucson or at least pretty close. Amen

* * * * * * *

A new young MD when doing his residency in OB, was quite embarrassed performing female pelvic exams. To cover his embarrassment he had unconsciously formed a habit of whistling softly. The middle-aged lady upon whom he was performing this exam suddenly burst out laughing and further embarrassed him. He looked up from his work and sheepishly said, "I'm sorry. Was I tickling you?" She replied, "No doctor, but the song you were whistling was 'I wish I was an Oscar Meyer Wiener.'"

* * * * * * *

At the beginning of my shift, I placed a stetho-scope on an elderly and slightly deaf female patient's anterior chest wall. "Big breaths," I instructed. "Yes, they used to be," remorsefully replied the patient.

* * * * * *

While acquainting myself with a new elderly patient, I asked, "How long have you been bed-ridden?" After a look of complete confusion, she answered, "Why, not for about twenty years—when my husband was alive."

ATTITUDE

The 92-year-old, petite, well-poised and proud lady, who is fully dressed each morning by eight o'clock, with her hair fashionably coifed and makeup perfectly applied, even though she is legally blind, moved to a nursing home today. Her husband of 70 years recently passed away, making the move necessary. After many hours of waiting patiently in the lobby of the nursing home, she smiled sweetly when told her room was ready. As she maneuvered her walker to the elevator, I provided a visual description of her tiny room, including the eyelet sheets that had been hung on her window. "I love it," she stated with the enthusiasm of an eight-year-old having just been presented with a new puppy. "Mrs. Jones, you haven't seen the room . . . just wait." "That doesn't have anything to do with it," she replied. "Happiness is something you decide on ahead of time. Whether I like my room or not doesn't depend on how the furniture is arranged... it's how I arrange my mind. I already decided to love it." "It's a decision I make every morning when I wake up. I have a choice; I can spend the day in bed recounting the difficulty I have with the parts of my body that no longer work, or get out of bed and be thankful for the ones that do. Each day is a gift, and as long as my eyes open, I'll focus on the new day and all the happy memories I've stored away... just for this time in my life. Old age is like a bank account... you withdraw from what you've put in."

So, my advice to you would be to deposit a lot of happiness in the bank account of
memories. Remember the five simple rules to be happy:
1. Free your heart from hatred.
2. Free your mind from worries.
3. Live simply.
4. Give more.
5. Expect less.

* * * * * * *

AFTER THREE PUTTS – BE CAREFUL

Recently I was golfing with a friend who had just bogeyed the fourth hole by three putting. With total frustration, he looked at me and said, "I would rather have my wife tell me that she was having an affair rather than three putt." My response, "Bill, what's said here will stay here."

* * * * * * *

PAINTINGS

Years ago, there was a very wealthy man who, with his devoted young son, shared a passion for art collecting. Together they traveled around the world, adding only the finest art treasures to their collection. Priceless works by Picasso, Van Gogh, Monet and many others adorned the walls of the family estate. The widowed elder man looked on with satisfaction, as his only child became an experienced art collector. The son's trained eye and sharp business mind caused his father to beam with pride as they dealt with art collectors around the world. As winter approached, war engulfed the nation, and the young man left to serve his country. After only a few short weeks, his father received a telegram. His beloved son was missing in action.

The art collector anxiously awaited more news, fearing he would never see his son again. Within days, his fears were confirmed. The young man had died while rushing a fellow soldier to a medic. Distraught and lonely, the old man faced the upcoming Christmas holidays with anguish and sadness. The joy of the season - a season that he and his son had so looked forward to would visit his house no longer.

On Christmas morning, a knock on the door awakened the depressed old man. As he walked to the door, the masterpieces of art on the walls only reminded him that his son was not coming home. As he opened the door, he was greeted by a soldier with a large package in his hand. He introduced himself to the man by saying, "I was a friend of your son. I was the one he was rescuing when he died. May I come in for a few moments? I have something to show you." As the two began to talk, the soldier told of how the man's son had told everyone of his father's love of fine art. "I'm an artist," said the soldier, "and I want to give you this."

As the old man unwrapped the package, the paper gave way to reveal a portrait of the man's son. Though the world would never consider it the work of a genius, the painting featured the young man's face in striking detail. Overcome with emotion, the man thanked the soldier, promising to hang the picture above the fireplace. A few hours later, after the soldier had departed, the old man set about his task. True to his word, the painting went above the fireplace, pushing aside thousands of dollars of paintings. And then the man sat in his chair and spent Christmas gazing at the gift he had been given.

During the days and weeks that followed, the man realized that even though his son was no longer with him, the boy's life would live on because of those he had touched. He would soon learn that his son had rescued dozens of wounded soldiers before a bullet stilled his caring heart. As the stories of his son's gallantry continued to reach him, fatherly pride and satisfaction began to ease the grief. The painting of his son soon became his most prized possession, far eclipsing any interest in the pieces for which museums around the world clamored. He told his neighbors it was the greatest gift he had ever received.

The following spring, the old man became ill and passed away. The art world was in anticipation. With the collector's passing, and his only son dead, those paintings would be sold at an auction. According to the will of the old man, all of the art works would be auctioned on Christmas day, the day he had received his greatest gift.

The day soon arrived and art collectors from around the world gathered to bid on some of the world's most spectacular paintings. Dreams would be fulfilled this day; greatness would be achieved, as many would claim, "I have the greatest collection."

The auction began with a painting that was not on any museum's list. It was the painting of the man's son. The auctioneer asked for an opening bid. The room was silent. "Who will open the bidding with $100?" he asked. Minutes passed. No one spoke. From the back of the room came, "Who cares about that painting? It's just a picture of his son. Let's forget it and go on to the good stuff." More voices echoed in agreement.

"No, we have to sell this one first," replied the auctioneer. "Now, who will take the son?" Finally, a friend of the old man spoke. "Will you take ten dollars for the painting? That's all I have. I knew the boy, so I'd like to have it." "I have ten dollars. Will anyone go higher?" called the auctioneer. After more silence, the auctioneer said, "Going once, going twice. Gone." The gavel fell.

Cheers filled the room and someone exclaimed, "Now we can get on with it and we can bid on these treasures!"

The auctioneer looked at the audience and announced the auction was over. Stunned disbelief quieted the room. Someone spoke up and asked, "What do you mean it's over? We didn't come here for a picture of some old guy's son. What about all of these paintings? There are millions of dollars of art here! I demand that you explain what's going on here!"

The auctioneer replied, "It's very simple. According to the will of the father, whoever takes the son... gets it all.

Puts things into perspective, doesn't it? Just as those art collectors discovered on that Christmas day, the message is still the same - the love of a Father - a Father whose greatest joy came from his son who went away and gave his life rescuing others. And because of that Father's love . . . whoever takes the Son gets it all.

* * * * * *

BEEP BEEP

One Saturday morning Grandpa took his young grandson on their weekly errands. The last stop was at the local bank. As the two stood in line to make a deposit, they both noticed at the same time that a very large lady was in line just ahead of them. I mean she was one big gal. Grandpa was praying that young Rob wouldn't make a comment about her size at least until they left the bank.

Just then, the fat lady's cell phone rang. "Ring-ring-ring." The young lad jumped backwards and looking up at his grandpa said, "Look out Gramps, she's going to back up."

* * * * * *

YOU'VE GOT TO BE KIDDING

A young man was driving between cities and because it was a beautiful autumn afternoon, he decided to take the back roads. As he drove slowly along he couldn't help but notice a nicely printed sign up ahead: "Sister of Mercy Convent & Brothel."

As he continued there was another sign saying the same thing, the only difference was this second sign said: "1 Mile Ahead." The third sign confirmed that the convent and brothel was ½ mile on the right.

Curiosity got the best of him so he pulled into the long driveway of the Sister of Mercy Convent & Brothel. As he approached the main building, a pleasant looking nun met him near the front entrance. Greetings were exchanged and he got right to the point. "Sister, I read your signs along the road. Are you really serious about this being a convent and a brothel?" The Sister replied, "Oh my yes, this is exactly as you read. We raise money in every way we can. We are a poor order of nuns and every little bit helps." Again, his curiosity was overwhelming and he asked her, rather sheepishly, "How much do you charge for one hour?" She answered, "one hour will be $50.00." He agreed to the price, paid her, and asked where he should go to be 'entertained.' The sister said, "Just go to the end of this long hall and go into the last door on the right and close the door behind you." The young man did as he was told. He entered the last room on the right and closed the door. He was shocked to find that he was standing outside not far from where his car was parked. As he looked around, he noticed a nicely printed fourth sign, "You have just been screwed by the Sisters of Mercy. Have a nice day!"

* * * * * *

TWO BETTER THAN ONE? DEPENDS

Maybe the old adage is true, "With age comes wisdom." My elderly parents used to go out for dinner quite often. They would always order just one entrée and split whatever it was down the middle. Half a dinner was plenty and both of them left full and happy.

But here comes the interesting part. Every time my wife and I drove over to their house and invited them out for "our treat" dinner—they each ordered their own separate meal. Yup, two full meals.

I guess what determines how hungry you are depends on who is picking up the check. Maybe another old adage is true—"like father, like son."

YOU KNOW YOU'RE IN ARIZONA
IN JULY WHEN...

- The trees are whistling for the dogs.

- The best parking space is determined by shade instead of distance.

- Hot water now comes out of both taps.

- You can make sun tea instantly.

- You learn that a seat belt buckle makes a pretty good branding iron.

- When the temperature drops below 95, you feel a little chilly.

- It only takes two fingers to steer the car.

- You can actually burn your hand opening the car door.

- You can find a parking spot next to the store you're going into.

- You ask the dog if he wants to go out to go potty and he look at you like, "Are you out of your mind?"

- You say to your spouse, "Do you realize we haven't been out of the house for three weeks?"

- You wake up at 6:30am and it's already in the 80's.

- You can go to a five star restaurant in shorts.

- You realize that bedtime in the winter is 10:00pm and in the summer at 10:00pm, you can actually sit on your patio.

- You look forward to seeing your "intelligent" neighbors who left for the summer and will return in October.

- Rattlers, scorpions, turkey buzzards, tarantulas, and fifty other somewhat poisonous spiders all together outnumber the total population of Arizona.

- The next jerk who says, "Ya, but it's a dry heat" is going to get punched right in the nose.

- The humidity, the property taxes and the ever-dreaded mosquitoes in the Midwest don't seem so bad after all. Or better still; spend six months in Pinetop, AZ.

- You can start cocktail hour anytime after 12 noon cause you doctor told you to push the fluids.

* * * * * * *

One fellow turned to his neighbor and said, "Don't know why they call them retirement communities- you have to work two jobs to afford to live there.

HOW FAST WE FORGET

86 year old George fell madly in love with 26 year old Buffy—a real cutie. Yup, you guessed it—George proposed, Buffy said, "yes" and the two were married.

It was mutually agreed that they would have separate bedroom. With his heart condition and his advanced years, it would be a wise thing to do. Well, their first night together, George kissed Buffy good night and retired to his bedroom and little Miss Cutie went into her room.

After about one hour, Buffy heard a tender tapping on her door and invited ol' George in. I guess making love is like riding a bike—you never forget how. George went back to his room with a smile. Forty-five minutes later, another knock on her door, and again another fifteen-minute visit by Mr. George.

These tender little episodes took place four times that night. On the fifth visit by ol' George, Buffy commented, "My goodness George, honey. I have never seen such stamina and strength in one night in all my life. You are truly amazing." George looked surprised and replied, "Oh, was I here before?"

* * * * * * *

GOLF FANATIC

It seems that this fellow went to Las Vegas and partied a little too hardy one evening. The next morning he awoke to find himself in bed with a totally unfamiliar female. The past evening was a total blur. The situation got even worse when the young lady informed him that the two of them had gotten married last evening.

Panic set in and he quickly jumped out of the bed and proceeded to explain that this whole thing was impossible, he couldn't be married to her, their "relationship" had to be annulled immediately. He further explained that he was a well-known golfer who was totally dedicated to the game of golf. He told her that he eats, sleeps and breathes golf 24 hours a day, "marriage just isn't in the picture." He told her she would not be happy with him.

She seemed to understand his explanation and said, "Well, as long as we're being honest with each other, I will admit that I'm a hooker."

Without hesitation he faced her head-on and said, "no problem, just rotate your left hand over slightly and that should take care of the problem."

* * * * * * *

FUN FACTS FOR EVERY DAY OF THE WEEK

Sunday: If a month begins on a Sunday, it will always have a Friday the 13th.

Monday: According to a study published by the British Medical Journal, 20% more people die from heart attacks on Monday than any other day.

Tuesday: A temporary employment agency found Tuesday is the most productive day of the week.

Wednesday: According to Paychex, Wednesday is the most common payday.

Thursday: This is the second most popular day of the week to eat out. Friday is the first.

Friday: This is the most preferred day to discharge or layoff employees because it gives them the weekend to recover

Saturday: Saturday is the most popular day for weddings.

* * * * * * *

Definition: "Intuition": It's that little voice within that keeps telling you you're right, despite the truth.

WHAT MY DAD TAUGHT ME ABOUT...

Religion: "You had better pray that comes out of the carpet.

Logic: "Because I said so, that's why."

Stamina: "You'll sit here until all that spinach is finished."

Meteorology: "It looks like a tornado hit your room."

The Circle of Life: "I brought you into this world, and I can take you out."

* * * * * * *

You know you're getting older when you're still a man or woman on the move but you're constantly out of breath.

* * * * * * *

Quip: I went into an antique store because the sign said, "We Have What Your Grandmother Threw Out." Sure enough, there was Grandpa.

* * * * * * *

One of my favorite signs in our church office: "For God so loved the world that He did not send a committee."

* * * * * * *

One of the hardest things to teach our children about money matters is that it does.

* * * * * * *

Everyone's mind goes blank occasionally, but only the smart ones remember to turn off the sound.

* * * * * * *

Life is a dance... by why are you the only one still doing the cha-cha?

* * * * * * *

The best way to make your car run better; check out the prices of new ones.

* * * * * * *

If pro is the opposite of con, then progress is the opposite of Congress.

* * * * * * *

You have to stand for what you believe in. Unless, of course, you believe in sitting down.

* * * * * * *

ALL HAPPY JOGGERS, PLEASE STAND UP
OOOPS, THERE ARE NONE

Webster defines "jogging" as "trotting steadily as a form of exercise." The definition I like best is for a word you might not use everyday—"joggle." This means "to shake or jolt." That best describes jogging in my book.

Don't get me wrong. I'm all for good, healthy exercise, and I walk everyday (weather permitting). But, I'm constantly reminded of the obvious difference between walkers and joggers.

First of all, joggers are all business. Once they get their spandex uniforms on, watch out. I think if I were to say to a jogger, "Hey, friend, your spouse was just taken to the emergency room," or "your house is on fire," the response might be, "Can't you see I'm jogging," as he/she joggles painfully away. Joggers are going to finish the course, come hell or high water.

On the other hand, there are several types of walkers. You have the retired strollers whose theme is, "Why hurry; enjoy the fresh air." Next, you have the handholding mates who just enjoy the outdoors and each other. There are the exercise-minded -- hip and arm swinging troopers who may tryout for the Olympics. We could also mention the teenage stone kickers who may get to wherever they are going by 2010. And, lastly, there are the dogs who are taking their owners for a walk. No matter which category you fall into, walkers are a friendly sort. They take time to greet a fellow walker; they smile and wave to the rest of the passing world. The activity isn't a chore.

Have you ever seen a relaxed or happy jogger, or one who is communicative? Do you know a jogger who isn't 100% intense? Not only are they physically, socially and emotionally fixed on the exercise project at hand, but moving cars, trucks and trains (maybe even planes) had better get out of the way.

I believe joggers are smarter than walkers. A runner knows the metric system, percentage of fat to body weight, names of exotic healthy herbs, fibers and other totally nutritious "stuff." They know all the appropriate food groups. The only groups I know are the folks we go out to dinner with. Joggers wear expensive wrist-watches so they don't arrive at a mile mark a second or two behind schedule. Punctuality is a virtue--ho hum. My only prerequisite-other than getting a good 45-minute walk in each day is to arrive home before cocktail hour.

I'd love to see joggers put on 10 to 15 pounds, get a little fleshy and "mellow out." A jogger friend of mine died of a heart attack. As we were paying our last respects, someone said, "Doesn't he look fit and trim and healthy?"

Heck, no, he doesn't -- he looks deader than my petunias.

I may not be as lean as a greyhound or have the body of that "Hasta la Vista, Baby" guy in California but, when I walk, I see birds, flowers, clouds and, best of all, I can greet everyone I meet along the way. Oh, one more thing, I'd sure like it if joggers were required to wear bells or some other warning device-- they scare the living bejebbers out of me when I don't hear or see them coming from behind.

* * * * * * *

DO ALL BRIDGE PLAYERS EAT QUICHE?

Did you ever stop to think of the number of card games you know how to play? Just think of it -- as a kid I'll bet you knew how to play such favorites as Old Maid, Rummy, Spit in the Ocean, War, Go Fish and 52-Card Pick Up. When you got a little older, you probably learned games like Solitaire, Poker, Royal and Michigan Rummy, Hearts, Spades, Crazy Eights, Black Jack and Uno. Bet you even know the game, "Oh ----."

My folks used to invite couples over to the house and play such games as Five Hundred, Euchre, Gin, Canasta, Sheepshead, Pinochle, and one of my favorites, Cribbage. See what I mean -- I have just listed about two dozen, and I'm sure we haven't even scratched the surface.

I bring up the subject of card games because I have just rewritten the rules for a very popular card game, a game that has become an institution in the U.S.A. I'm speaking of the game of bridge. I am going to try my best not to come across as closed minded to this game that some treat as a religion. I will not, nor would I ever, infer that bridge players can't play their game and smile, talk, chew gum, or even act like they're enjoying themselves.

My wife belonged to a bridge club (and I use the term loosely). The first 13 years they played serious bridge. For the last 20 years, all they did was talk and eat desserts. I would much prefer to commune with five other gentlemen around a felt-covered table and play a jolly game of poker.

Now for the new rules for my least favorite game. If I could play bridge by these rules, I'd have a ball. Are you ready? Here we go.

1. Pick up your cards as dealt. You will be ready to bid ahead of the others.

2. If your hand is rotten, mention it. It will guide your partner in his/her bid and play.

3. If your partner bids first, don't hesitate to raise. He has to play it.

4. Never hurry. Try several cards on a trick until you are sure which one you prefer.

5. Occasionally ask what is trump. It will show you are interested in the game.

6. Don't show lack of interest when you're dummy. Help your partner out with suggestions.

7. Walk around the table when you are dummy and look at the other hands. Tell them what cards are good and how many tricks they can take if they play right.

8. Talk about other subjects during the game. It makes for good fellowship.

9. Feel free to criticize your partner. He will do much better as a result.

10. Always trump your partner's trick. Never take a chance.

11. Don't try to remember the rules. It is too confusing.

12. If it is a money game, always stop when you're ahead. It will leave a lasting impression and folks will remember you.

13. Always explain your plays, particularly when you are set. It shows card knowledge.

14. Disagree with established rules and conventions. People will know you are a person of independent mind.

15. If holding poor cards, expose an honor and demand a new deal.

16. Eat chocolate caramels or other adhesive candy while playing. It keeps the cards from skidding.

There now, anybody ready to play?

* * * * * * *

"LET'S SEE WHAT SHE'LL DO"

Ron had just picked up his brand new Porsche Convertible from the dealership and because it was a perfect afternoon, he decided to head out into the countryside and test his new toy. The car was perfect, had all the latest bells and whistles and the speedometer went up to 160 mph.

He was alone on the backroads and he couldn't resist the temptation—"let's see what she'll do." Ron eased the Porsche up to 90 mph with no problem at all. He gave it a little more and was cruising along at a cool 100mph.

Something caught his eye coming from behind. Yup, it was a police officer with his lights on and the siren at full blast. Without thinking of the consequences, Ron pushed down on the gas peddle and the car responded. So did the squad car. In a split second, Ron thought to himself, "What in the world am I doing. I must have lost my mind for a second. I better pull over."

The officer approached the driver's side and with a dry smile greeted the now nervous driver. "In a hurry young man?" Ron was caught red handed. He assured the officer that this certainly was not the way he normally drove. He just got caught up in the moment.

The officer told Ron that he clocked him at an even 120mph. Ron took a deep breath and politely said, "I know you are just doing your job officer but just this once could you please give me a warning ticket?" The officer thought a minute, smiled, and said, "Well, it is a Friday afternoon and I sure don't want to be doing a lot of paperwork and because I'm off the next two weeks, I don't want to have to appear in court. Ok, I'll tell you what I'll do. If you can give me a good reason why you were going 120mph – and I mean a real good reason- one I haven't heard before- I'll let you off with a warning ticket."

Without hesitation, Ron looked up at the officer and in a very sincere voice said, "You see officer, just one month ago today my wife ran away with a police officer. When I saw you coming up behind me with your lights and siren on, I figured you had her in the car with you and you were chasing me so you could return her. That's why I stepped it up to 120mph." The officer grinned and said, "Here's your warning ticket sir, have a nice day."

* * * * * * *

OLE, LENA AND SVEN

Scene I

Every morning at 6:30 sharp, Ole and Lena sat at their breakfast table and ate leftover lutefisk and lefse for breakfast while they listened to the kitchen radio. It was the middle of January and the snow she was a blowin' don't ja know dere. Ole was anxious to hear the updated local weather report. "OK now Lena, be real quiet cause he's givin' da weather report." The report told them that because of the heavy snowfall everybody was to park their cars on the even side of the street so that the plows could plow the snow on the odd side. Being an obedient citizen, Ole put on his parka and moved his car to the even side of the street.

The next morning the same scene. Ole told Lena, "Ya Lena, you make the best lefse this side of Fargo don't ja know." As usual, the weather report was the highlight of their morning. "Today we want you folks to move your cars to the odd side of the street so the plows can clean up the snow," etc. etc. etc. As the day before, Ole started the car and drove it to the odd side of the street as he was told to do.

The third morning as the two ate their Krumkake and Sandbakkels the weather had taken a real turn for the worst and the radio reception was scratchy at best and very hard to under-

135

stand. Ole had his ear right up to the cloth front of the radio and he was straining to get the updated weather and parking information. Just as the announcer was about to give his report the radio went dead. "Lena, we missed the weather and parking report. What do we do now?" Lena thought for a minute and said, "Ole, why don't you just leave the car in the garage like it has been all night?"

Scene II

As they sat finishing their breakfast, Lena said, "Ya know Ole, I haven't seen old Tom Cat for two days now. With dis weather as bad as it is, I'm kinda worried about old Tom. Maybe you should go out lookin' for him." After his third cup of coffee Ole put on his parka and went out into the back yard. He called several times but no Tom cat. Finally, Ole noticed something over behind the garage. Yup, it was old Tom Cat frozen stiffer than a board. Ole went into the garage, got his pick and shovel and dug a hole in the back yard to bury old Tom.

Just as he was about to put old Tom in his final resting place, Sven, their next-door neighbor, stuck his head over the fence. "Hey der Ole, whatcha doen?" Ole said, "Take off your cap, Sven and hold it over your heart—dis is a funeral dontcha know." As Sven did as he was told in a most reverent manner, Ole held old Tom by the tail and in his most serious Lutheran voice said, "In da name of da Father and da Son, and in-da-hole-he-goes."

Scene III

After old Tom was laid to rest, Ole and Sven stood there talking. Sven said, "Ole, I have something to say to you and I hope you take it the right way." "What is it, Sven?" Sven went on, "well Ole, Saturday night about 9:00 I was out walking on the front sidewalk. It was all dark and everything and as I passed your house I looked up and I seen you and Lena upstairs in da bedroom—you know—making whoopee and stuff. You should pull the blinds down Ole if you and Lena are going to—well, you know what I mean." Ole looked at his pal Sven and laughed and said, "Ha ha, the yoke is on you Sven, I wasn't even home on Saturday night."

* * * * * * *

It seems that old Hans died. So Helga went into the local newspaper office to run the obituary in the paper. Helga told the man behind the counter what she wanted to do and he asked, "What did you want to have printed?" Helga said, "Just say – 'Hans died'." The editor said, "Surely you want to say more than that. In fact Helga, we have a five word minimum." Helga thought for a minute and then said, "OK, print this, 'Hans died-boat for sale'."

* * * * * * *

A PRAYER FOR LATER YEARS

Lord, Thou knowest that I am growing older. Keep me from becoming too talkative, and particularly keep me from falling into the tiresome habit of expressing an opinion on every subject.

Release me from the craving to straighten out everybody's affairs. Keep my mind free from the recital of endless details. Give me wings to get to the point.

Give me grace, dear Lord to listen to others describe their aches and pains. Help me endure the boredom with patience and keep my lips sealed, for my own aches and pains are increasing in number and intensity, and the pleasure of discussing them is becoming sweeter as the years go by.

Teach me the glorious lesson that, occasionally, I might be mistaken. Keep me reasonably sweet. I do not wish to be a saint (saints are so hard to live with), but a sour old person is the work of the devil.

Make me thoughtful, but not moody; helpful, but not pushy; independent, yet able to accept with graciousness favors that others wish to bestow on me.

Free me of the notion that simply because I have lived a long time, I am wiser than those who have not lived so long.

If I do not approve of some of the changes that have taken place in recent years, give me the wisdom to keep my mouth shut.

Lord knows that when the end comes, I would like to have a friend or two left.

* * * * * * *

TELL IT LIKE IT IS

Father Mike was instructing the young alter boy. "When its time during the mass for you to light the candles on the alter, I will chant (sing) the following words, 'and the angel lit the candles.' When you hear me sing those words, you come in from the small room behind the alter and light the candles."

When Mass had started the priest chanted, "And the Angel lit the candles." Nothing happened. Again, the priest sang, "And the Angel lit the candles." This went on three more times and still no alter boy. Finally a voice sang loud and clear from behind the alter, "And the cat peed on the matches."

* * * * * * *

WORD GAME TEST

Oh yes, here are the answers to the test found on pages 91-92:

1.   7 – days of the week
2.   12 – signs of the zodiac
3.   1001 – Arabian nights
4.   54 – Cards in a deck (with Joker)
5.   9 – planets in the solar system
6.   88 – keys on a piano
7.   13 – stripes on the American flag
8.   32 – degrees Fahrenheit at which water freezes
9.   18 – holes on a golf course
10. 90 – degrees in a right angle
11. 8 – sides on a STOP sign
12. 3 – Blind mice (see how they run)
13. 4 – quarts in a gallon
14. 24 – hours in a day
15. 1 – wheel on a unicycle
16. 5 – digits in a Zip Code
17. 57 – Heinz Varieties
18. 11 – players on a football team
19. 1000 – words that a picture is worth
20. 29 – days in February in a Leap Year
21. 64 – squares on a Checker Board

22. 40 – days and nights of the great flood
23. 76 – trombones in the Big Parade
24. 50 – ways to leave your lover
25. 99 – bottles of beer on the wall
26. 9 – judges on the Supreme Court
27. 7 – Brides for Seven Brothers
28. 21 – dots on a die
29. 1 – horn on a unicorn
30. 60 – seconds in a minute
31. 200 – dollars to pass "GO" in Monopoly

* * * * * * *

Here is my favorite "Senility Prayer:"

Dear God,
Please give me the Senility to forget the people
I never liked anyway---
The good fortune to run into the
people I do like---
And the eyesight to tell the difference
AMEN

* * * * * * *

Everybody should pay his income tax with a smile. I tried it but they wanted cash. Speaking about income tax, one lady called the IRS and asked if birth control pills were deductible. Only if they don't work, she was told.

* * * * * * *

SENIOR CITIZEN CHUCKLES

Two old fellows went out for a walk. The first one says, "Windy isn't it?" The second one says, "No, it's Thursday."

* * * * * * *

Morris, an 84-year-old man went to his doctor for a physical. A few days later, the doctor saw Morris walking down the street with a gorgeous young lady on his arm. The doc introduced himself to the young lady and said to Morris, "You're really doing great, aren't you?" Morris replied, "Just doing what you told me to do, Doc: get a hot mamma and be cheerful," The doc said, "I didn't say that Morris. I said you got a heart murmur. Be careful."

* * * * * * *

An elderly gent was invited to his old friends' home one evening for dinner. He was impressed by the way his buddy addressed his wife in very sincere and endearing terms— Honey, My Love, Darling, Sweetheart, Pumpkin, etc. While the wife was in the kitchen the guest said to the host, "I think it's wonderful that after all these years, you still call your wife those loving pet names." The old man got a sheepish look on his face and said, "I have to tell you the truth. I forgot her name about ten years ago."

* * * * * * *

The big secret of staying young is to find an age that you really like and stick to it. Now you've got it baby—stay with what's working.

* * * * * * *

By the time a man learns to behave himself, he's too old to do anything else.

Adam and Eve said, "Lord, when we were in the garden, you walked with me every day. Now we never see you anymore and we are lonesome." And God said, "No problem! I will create a companion for you that will be with you forever and who will be a reflection of my great love for you. Regardless of how selfish or childish or unlovable you may be, this new companion will accept you as you are and will love you as I do, in spite of yourselves.

And God created a new animal to be their companion. And it was a good animal. And God was greatly pleased. And Adam said, "Lord, I do not know what to name this tail wagging animal." And God said, "No problem! Because this new animal will reflect my love for you, his name will be close to my name and you shall call him 'DOG'."

After awhile, it came to pass that an angel came to the Lord and said, "Adam and Eve have become filled with pride. They strut and preen like peacocks and they believe they are worthy of adoration. DOG has indeed taught them that they are loved but perhaps too well." And God said, "No problem! I will create for them another new animal who will forever remind them of their limitations, so they will know that they are not always worthy of adoration."

And God created CAT to be with Adam and Eve. And CAT would not obey them. When Adam and Eve gazed into CAT's eyes, they were reminded that they were not at all the supreme beings. And Adam and Eve learned humility. And they were greatly improved. And God was pleased. And DOG was happy. And CAT didn't give a damn one way or the other.

* * * * * * *

CATS OF COURSE

"And thou shall have dominion over all the beasts...except, of course, for cats."

Felines 12:15

* * * * * * *

Men are from earth. Women are from earth. Deal with it.

SMUCKERS IS BETTER

Not long ago, Ed and Jean drove to Denver to see Jean's elderly mother. After a good nights sleep they got up the next morning to a table all set for one of Mom's farm style breakfasts.

Ed and Jean looked at each other with a questioning smile at what they saw next to Mom's place setting—a tube of K-Y Jelly. Jean asked Mom what that tube was there for. She said,

"Oh that. It was cheaper than Smuckers Strawberry Jelly but I really don't like it nearly as well on my toast. When the tube is gone, I'm going back to Smuckers. Maybe you two would prefer peanut butter."

* * * * * * *

Eat well, drink before dinner, stay fit, and die anyway.

* * * * * * *

A balanced diet is a cookie in each hand.

* * * * * * *

The best way to stay young is to eat right, exercise and lie about your age.

* * * * * * *

GOD TRULY DOES HAVE A SENSE OF HUMOR

These are things that God might say to each one of us:

- Let's meet at my house Sunday before the game.

- Come on over and bring the kids.

- What part of "Thou Shalt Not" don't you understand?

- We need to talk.

- Keep using my name in vain and I'll see that you never get a parking spot.

- That "Love Thy Neighbor" thing ... I mean it.

- Big Bang Theory, you've go to be kidding.

- Need directions?

- You think it's hot in Arizona in July?

- Have you read my #1 best seller? There will be a test.

- Don't make me come down there!

* * * * * * *

Always yield to temptation, because it may not pass your way again.

HIGH FLYING HUMOR

While taxiing the crew of US Air flight departing Ft. Lauderdale made a wrong turn and came nose to nose with a United 727 aircraft.

The irate female ground controller lashed out at the US Air crew, screaming, "US Air 2343, where are you going? I told you to turn right onto Charlie runway. You turned right on Delta! STOP right there. I know it's difficult for you to tell the difference between C's and D's, but try to get it right!"

Continuing her tirade to the embarrassed crew, she was now shouting hysterically: "God, you have screwed everything up? It will take forever to sort this mess out! You stay right where you are and don't move until I tell you to! I'll tell you what I want you to do in about half an hour. I want you to go exactly where I tell you, when I tell you, and how I tell you! You got that US Air 2343?"

"Yes Ma'am" the humbled pilot responded. The ground control frequency went totally dead after the verbal bashing of US Air 2343. No flight crew in the area wanted to engage the irate ground controller in her current state of mind. Tension in every cockpit was running high. Then an unknown pilot broke the silence and asked, "Wasn't I married to you once?"

* * * * * * *

A DC 10 had an exceedingly long and fast roll-out after landing well down the runway. San Jose Tower responded: "American 751, turn right at the end of the runway, if you are able. If not able, take the Guadalupe exit off Highway 101 and make a right at the light and follow the signs back to the airport."

* * * * * * *

KNOCK-KNOCK

The new Bishop was visiting in the homes of parish members. At one house, it seemed rather obvious that someone was at home, but no answer came to his repeated knocks at the door. He took out one of his cards and wrote "Revelation 3:20" on the back and left it in the door. When the tithing envelopes were opened and processed the following Sunday, he found that his card had been returned. Added to it was this Biblical message, "Genesis 3:10."

Reaching for his bible to check out the exact citation, he broke out in raucous laughter. Revelation 3:20 begins, "Behold, I stand at the door and knock."

Genesis 3:10 reads, "I heard thy voice and I hid myself for I was naked."

A MAJOR LEAGUE PUT DOWN

One evening my wife and I were about to have an exquisite dinner at a Five Star Restaurant in San Francisco. As we waited in the foyer for the maitre'd to seat us, I couldn't help but notice a rather large well-dressed woman waiting for her husband who was finalizing their dinner bill.

The foyer was elegant in every detail. On a rather expensive looking table was a large glass

dish with individually wrapped Godiva Chocolates. While waiting for her husband this broad
beamed female positioned herself between the
folks in the lobby and the Godiva goodies. She
looked both ways to make sure no one saw her
putting a couple large handfuls into her purse.

Just at that very moment, the maitre'd said
from across the foyer for all of the patrons to
hear, "Ma'am, I beg your pardon, Ma'am, yes
you in the lovely purple evening dress. Would
you like a bag for those chocolates so you won't
have to fill your purse?"

Well, she deposited the third handful back into
the bowl and retreated to the front entrance to
wait for dear sweet hubby. Red faced and red
handed she'd been caught with her fat paws in
the candy dish. Don't you just love it?

* * * * * * *

MY TOOT'S SHORES CAPER

One of my favorite restaurants in all the world
was Toot's Shores in New York City. It was the
fall of 1967 and I was entertaining five business
clients for dinner that evening. As the six of us
sat comfortably around our table enjoying our
cocktails and fancy hors d'oeuvres one of my
guests asked our waiter for an ashtray. The
smoothly professional waiter promptly brought
our table a clean, beautiful ashtray. I say

"beautiful" because it was an artfully designed maroon ceramic ashtray with the name of the restaurant and its logo artfully displayed. I had to have one of these to take back to Wisconsin as a souvenir. But how could I pull this off without getting caught or being embarrassed in front of my guests?

I had a plan—not to dishonestly acquire this object of art- but to tactfully bribe our well-seasoned waiter.

I excused myself from my guests in order to visit the Men's Room. I approached our waiter as nonchalantly as I could and told him I wanted to have one of those Toot's Shore ash-trays. I'd be happy to make it worth his while. He nodded knowingly and suggested, "After you return to your table just motion for me to come over. Tell me that your table napkin was soiled and that you would like me to bring you a clean napkin. If you want, you could have a ten dollar bill in the soiled napkin and I'll have a new, clean ashtray tucked under the new napkin." Perfect, the plan was set into motion.

"Waiter, over here, may I please have a clean napkin, mine is soiled?" "Why of course Sir, I'll be right back." The exchange was made without a flaw. I had my ashtray, he had his ten bucks, and no one was the wiser.

As we finished our dinner, dessert and coffee, one of my guest called our waiter over to our table, "Ah yes young man, I'm wondering if you would be kind enough to bring three or four of your ash trays for us to take home as souvenirs?" Without hesitation, the waiter got five new ashtrays and gave one to each of my guests, "Compliments of the house, Gentlemen, no charge. Enjoy the rest of your evening."

As we left our seating area the waiter looked my way as if to say, "Hope you enjoy your ashtray, farm boy."

* * * * * * *

A wise, and rich man once said, "Always borrow money from a pessimist. He won't expect to get paid back.

NONE OF YOUR DAMN BUSINESS

Recently I flew to Madison, WI, to visit my 94-year-old Dad. I could relate several humorous happenings over the four-day visit but I'll share just one that struck my funny bone.

Dad took me down to the dining room to have dinner one of the evenings. This is a very lovely assisted living retirement home. Anyway, we got down to the dining room at 4:30pm. Everybody sits in the same seat at the same table every evening—no exceptions.

Every one of the six people at "Dad's table" was hard of hearing; actually, they were all deaf. During dinner, the elderly gentleman sitting next to me looked across the table and said in a loud voice to the man across from him, "Louis, why don't you eat your asparagus?" Louis responded, "I didn't order a sandwich and it's none of your damn business anyway."

Fact is, they didn't even have asparagus that evening. Oh well!

* * * * * * *

X-RATED

"Clinton did it between the Bushes."

* * * * * * *

Leroy met his friend Vern on the street and asked, "How was your vacation last year?" Vern replied, "Well, Leroy you suggested that Niagara Falls was a beautiful place to go, but guess what happened? Molly got pregnant. Then this year you told me that the Grand Canyon was a spectacular vacation spot. And yup, you guessed it, Molly got pregnant again." "What do you have planned for this coming summer?" Vern replied, "This year I'm going to do something real different—this year it's going to be on the beach in Florida." Leroy asked, "What's so different about going to Florida for your vacation?" Vern answered, "This year I'm taking Molly with me."

* * * * * *

Here's another chance to jot a note to the cheap so-and-so who borrowed this book. Next time, RENT it to him!

Great Truths About Life That Little Children Have Learned

- You can't put an apple in your neighbor's toilet.

- No matter how hard you try, you can't baptize cats.

- When your Mom is mad at your Dad, don't let her brush your hair.

- If your sister hits you, don't hit her back. They always catch the second person.

- Never ask a 3-year old to hold a tomato.

- You can't trust dogs to watch your food.

- Don't sneeze when someone is cutting your hair.

- Puppies still have bad breath even after eating a Tic- Tac.

- School lunches stick to the wall.

- You can't hide a piece of broccoli in a glass of milk.

- Don't wear polka-dot underwear under white shorts.

Great Truths About Life That
Adults Have Learned

- There's always a lot to be thankful for if you take time to look for it. For example, I am sitting here thinking how nice it is that wrinkles don't hurt.

- Reason to smile: Every seven minutes of every day, someone in an aerobics class pulls a hamstring.

- Families are like fudge...mostly sweet with a few nuts.

- Middle age is when you choose cereal for the fiber, not the toy.

- The more you complain the longer God lets you live.

- If you can remain calm, you don't have all the facts.

- You know you're getting old when you stoop to tie your shoes and wonder what else you can do while you're down there.

PROOF POSITIVE

THREE PROOFS THAT JESUS WAS PUERTO RICAN

1. His first name was Jesus.
2. He was bilingual.
3. He was always being harassed by the authorities

THREE PROOFS THAT JESUS WAS BLACK

1. He called everybody "brother."
2. He liked Gospel.
3. He couldn't get a fair trial.

THREE PROOFS THAT JESUS WAS JEWISH

1. He went into his father's business.
2. He lived at home until he was 33.
3. He was sure his Mother was a virgin, and his Mother was sure he was God.

THREE PROOFS THAT JESUS WAS ITALIAN

1. He talked with his hands.
2. He had wine with every meal.
3. He worked in the building trades.

THREE PROOFS THAT JESUS WAS A CALIFORNIAN

1. He never cut his hair.
2. He walked around barefoot.
3. He started a new religion.

THREE PROOFS THAT JESUS WAS IRISH

1. He never got married.
2. He was always telling stories.
3. He loved green pastures.

(And now the MOST Compelling EVIDENCE)

THREE PROOFS THAT JESUS WAS A WOMAN

1. He had to feed a crowd, at a moment's notice, when there was no food.
2. He kept trying to get the message across to a bunch of men who just didn't get it.
3. Even when he was dead, he had to get up because there was more work for him to do.

WORLD'S SHORTEST BOOKS

15. MY PLAN TO FIND THE REAL KILLERS - by O. J. Simpson

14. THINGS I WOULD NOT DO FOR MONEY - by Dennis Rodman

13. THE WILD YEARS - by Al Gore

12. AMELIA EARHART'S GUIDE TO THE PACIFIC OCEAN

11. AMERICA'S MOST POPULAR LAWYERS

10. DETROIT - A TRAVEL GUIDE

9. DR. KEVORKIAN'S COLLECTION OF MOTIVATIONAL SPEECHES

8. EVERYTHING MEN KNOW ABOUT WOMEN

7. EVERYTHING WOMEN KNOW ABOUT MEN

6. GEORGE FOREMAN'S BIG BOOK OF BABY NAMES

5. TO ALL THE MEN I'VE LOVED BEFORE - by Ellen DeGeneres

4. MIKE TYSON'S GUIDE TO DATING ETIQUETTE

3. SPOTTED OWL RECIPES - by the EPA

2. THE AMISH PHONE DIRECTORY

And the World's number one shortest book...

1. THE BOOK OF VIRTUES
   - by Bill Clinton

* * * * * * *

And God created woman and she had three breasts. He then asked woman "Is there anything you'd like to have changed?" She replied, "Yes, could you get rid of this middle breast?" And so it was done, and it was good. Then the woman exclaimed as she was holding that third breast in her hand, "What can be done with this useless boob?" And God created Man.

* * * * * * *

WHERE WAS I?

Three older ladies were discussing the travails of getting older. One said, "Sometimes I catch myself with a jar of mayonnaise in my hand in front of the refrigerator and can't remember whether I need to put it away or start making a sandwich." The second lady added, "Yes, sometimes I find myself on the landing of the stairs and can't remember whether I was on my way up or on my way down." The third one responded, "Well, I'm glad I don't have that problem, knock on wood," as she rapped her knuckles on the table, then told them, "That must be the door, I'll get it!"

* * * * * * *

The Conservative Little Girl

A first grade teacher explains to her class that she is a liberal Democrat. She asks her students to raise their hands if they were liberal Democrats too. Not really knowing what a liberal Democrat was but wanting to be like their teacher, their hands explode into the air like fleshy fireworks.

There is, however, one exception. A girl named Lucy has not gone along with the crowd. The teacher asks her why she has decided to be different. "Because I'm not a liberal Democrat" Replies Lucy. "Then," asks the teacher, "What are you?" "Why I'm a proud conservative Republican," boasts the little girl. The teacher is a little perturbed now, her face slightly red. She asks Lucy why she is a conservative Republican. "Well, I was brought up to trust in myself instead of relying on an intrusive government to care for me and do all of my thinking. My Dad and Mom are conservative Republicans, and I am a conservative Republican too." The teacher is now angry. "That's no reason," she says loudly. "What if your Mom was a moron and your dad was a idiot. What would you be then?" A pause and a smile... "Then," says Lucy, "I'd be a liberal Democrat."

* * * * * * *

READY FOR ANOTHER BLONDE JOKE?

A blonde decides to try horseback riding, even though she has had no lessons or prior experience. She mounts the horse, unassisted, and the horse immediately springs into motion. It gallops along at a steady and rhythmic pace, but the blonde begins to slip from the saddle. In terror, she grabs for the horse's mane, but cannot seem to get a firm grip. She tries to throw her arms around the horse's neck, but she slides down the side of the horse anyway. The horse gallops along, seemingly impervious to its slipping rider. Finally, giving up her frail grip, the blonde attempts to leap away from the horse and throw herself to safety. Unfortunately, her foot has become entangled in the stirrup, and she; is now at the mercy of the horse's pounding hooves as her head is struck against the ground over and over. As her head is battered against the ground, she is mere moments away from unconsciousness when to her great fortune. . . Frank, the Wal-Mart greeter, sees her and unplugs the horse.

* * * * * * *

In the rest room an accountant, a lawyer and a cowboy were standing side-by-side using the urinal. The accountant finished, zipped up and started washing and literally scrubbing his hands...clear up to his elbows...he used about 20 paper towels before he finished. He turned to the other two men and commented, "I graduated from the University of Michigan, we were taught to be clean." The lawyer finished, zipped up and quickly wet the tips of his fingers, grabbed one paper towel and commented," I graduated from Stanford and they taught us to be environmentally conscious." The cowboy zipped up and as he was walking out the door said, "I graduated from the University of Arizona and they taught us not to pee on our hands.

* * * * * * *

FUNNY NOTES

Dear Hallie,
I have a man I never could trust. He cheats so much. I'm not even sure this baby I'm carrying is his.

Dear Karen,
I am a twenty-three-year-old liberated woman who has been on the pill for two years. It's getting expensive and I think my boy friend should

share half the cost, but I don't know him well enough to discuss money with him.

Dear Ginny,
I suspected that my husband had been fooling around, and when I confronted him with the evidence, he denied everything and said it would never happen again.

Dear Mary,
Our son writes that he is taking Judo. Why would a boy who was raised in a good Christian home turn against his own religion?

Dear Charlotte,
I joined the Navy to see the world. I've seen it. Now how do I get out?

Dear Sydney,
My forty-year-old son has been paying a psychiatrist $50 an hour every week for two-and-a-half years. He must be crazy.

Dear Betty,
My mother is mean and short-tempered. I think she is going through her mental pause.

Dear Norma,
You told some woman whose husband had lost all interest in sex to send him to a doctor. Well, my husband lost all interest in sex years ago and he is a doctor.

Dear Pat,
I have always wanted to have my family history traced, but I can't afford to spend a lot of money to do it. Any suggestions? Sam

Dear Sam,
Yes. Run for public office.

Dear Doris,
I am forty-four-years old and I would like to meet a man my age with no bad habits. Rose

Dear Rose,
So would I.

* * * * * * *

THE MALE SPECIES

Because I'm a man, when I lock my keys in the car I will fiddle with a wire clothes hanger and ignore your suggestions that we call a road service until long after hypothermia has set in.

Because I'm a man, when the car isn't running very well, I will pop the hood and stare at the engine as if I know what I'm looking at. If another man shows up, one of us will say to the other, "I used to be able to fix these things, but now with all these computers and everything, I wouldn't know where to start."

Because I'm a man, when I catch a cold I need someone to bring me soup and take care of me while I lie in bed and moan. You never get as sick as I do.

Because I'm a man, I can be relied upon to purchase basic groceries at the store, like milk or bread, I cannot be expected to find exotic items like "Cumin" or "Tofu." For all I know these are the same thing.

Because I'm a man, when one of our appliances stops working, I will insist on taking it apart, despite evidence that this will just cost me twice as much once the repair person gets here and has to put it back together.

Because I'm a man, I don't think we're all that lost, and no, I don't think we should stop and ask someone. Why would you listen to a complete stranger? I mean, how the heck could he know where we're going?

Because I'm a man, there is no need to ask me what I'm thinking about. The answer is always either sex or food, though I have to make up something else when you ask, so don't.

Because I'm a man, I do not want to visit your mother, or have your mother come visit us, or talk to her when she calls, or think about her any more than I have to. Whatever you got her for Mother's Day is okay. I don't need to see it.

And don't forget to pick up something for my Mom, too.

Because I'm a man, you don't have to ask me if I liked the movie. Chances are if you're crying at the end of it, I didn't.

Because I'm a man, I think what you're wearing is fine. I thought what you were wearing five minutes ago was fine, too. Either pair of shoes is fine. With the belt or without it looks fine. Your hair is fine. You look fine. Can we just go now?

Because I'm a man, and this is, after all, the 21st Century, I will share equally in the housework. You just do the laundry, the cooking, the gardening, the cleaning, and the dishes. I'll do the rest.

* * * * * * *

So, how's your day going?

EXPRESSIONS FOR A WOMAN'S HIGH STRESS DAYS

1. You! Off my planet!
2. Not the brightest crayon in the box now, are we.
3. Well, this day was a total waste of makeup.

4. Errors have been made. Others will be blamed.

5. And your crybaby, whiny opinion would be...?

6. I'm not crazy; I've just been in a very bad mood for 30 years.

7. Allow me to introduce my selves.

8. Sarcasm is just one more service we offer.

9. Whatever kind of look you were going for, you missed.

10. Do they ever shut up on your planet?

11. I'm just working here till a good fast-food job opens up.

12. I'm trying to imagine you with a personality.

13. Stress is when you wake up screaming and you realize you haven't fallen asleep yet.

14. I can't remember if I'm the good twin or the evil one.

15. How many times do I have to flush before you go away?

16. I just want revenge. Is that so wrong?

17. You say I'm a bitch like it's a bad thing.

18. Can I trade this job for what's behind door #2?

19. Nice perfume. Must you marinate in it?

20. Chaos, panic & disorder - my work here is done.

21. Everyone thinks I'm psychotic, except for my friends deep inside the earth.

22. Earth is full. Go home.

23. Is it time for your medication or mine?

24. Aw, did I step on your poor little bitty ego?

25. How do I set a laser printer to stun?

26. I'm not tense, just terribly, terribly alert.

27. When I want your opinion, I'll give it to you.

SOUND FAMILIAR?

Golfer: "That can't be my ball, caddy. It looks far too old."
Caddy: "It's a long time since we started, sir."

Golfer: "Do you think I can get there with a 5-iron?"
Caddy: "Eventually."

Golfer: "You've got to be the worst caddy in the world!" he screamed.
Caddy: "I doubt it," replied the caddy. "That would be too much of a coincidence."

Golfer: "I've played so poorly all day; I think I'm going to go drown myself in that lake."

Caddy: "I don't think you could keep your head down that long."

Golfer: "I'd move heaven and earth to be able to break 100 on this course."
Caddy: "Try heaven," advised the caddy. "You've already moved most of the earth."

Golfer: "This is the worst golf course I've ever played on!"
Caddy: "This isn't the golf course, sir! We left that an hour ago."

Golfer: Well Caddy, How do you like my game?"
Caddy: "Very good, sir! But personally, I prefer golf."

Golfer: "Well, I have never played this badly before."
Caddy: "I didn't realize you had played before, sir."

Golfer: "Caddy, do you think my game is improving?"
Caddy: "Oh yes, sir! You miss the ball much closer than you used to."

Golfer: "Please stop checking your watch all the time, Caddy. It's distracting."
Caddy: "This isn't a watch, Sir. It's a compass!"

Golfer: "Caddy, do you think it is a sin to play golf on Sunday?"
Caddy: "The way you play, Sir, it's a crime any day of the week."

Golfer: "This golf is a funny game."
Caddy: "It's not supposed to be."

* * * * * * *

WHEN I'M AN OLD LADY

When I'm an old lady, I'll live with my kids, and make their life happy and filled with such fun. I want to pay back all the joy they've provided, returning each deed. Oh, they'll be so excited.
...When I'm an old lady and live with my kids.

I'll write on the wall with red, white, and blue; and bounce on the furniture wearing my shoes. I'll drink from the carton and then leave it out. I'll stuff all the toilets and oh, they'll shout.
...When I'm an old lady and live with my kids.

When they're on the phone and just out of reach, I'll get into things like sugar and bleach. Oh, they'll snap their fingers and then shake their head, and when that is done, I'll hide under the bed.
...When I'm an old lady and live with my kids.

When they cook dinner and call me to meals,
I'll not eat my green beans or salads congealed.
I'll gag on my okra, spill milk on the table,
and when they get angry, run fast as I'm able
...When I'm an old lady and live with my kids.

I'll sit close to the TV, through the channels I'll
click. I'll cross both my eyes to see if they stick.
I'll take off my socks and throw one away,
and play in the mud until the end of the day
...When I'm an old lady and live with my kids.

And later in bed, I'll lay back and sigh,
and thank God in prayer and then close my
eyes; and my kids will look down with a smile
slowly creeping, and say with a groan, "She's so
sweet when she's sleeping."
...When I'm an old lady and live with my kids.

* * * * * * *

NEW BARBIE DOLLS

Finally, a Barbie I can relate to! At long last,
here are some NEW Barbie dolls to coincide
with OUR aging gracefully:

1. Bifocals Barbie. Comes with her own set
    of blended-lens fashion frames in six wild
    colors (half-frames too!), neck chain and
    large-print editions of Vogue and Martha
    Stewart Living.

2. Hot Flash Barbie. Press Barbie's belly button and watch her face turn beet red while tiny drops of perspiration appear on her forehead. Comes with hand-held fan and tiny tissues.

3. Facial Hair Barbie. As Barbie's hormone levels shift, see her whiskers grow. Available with teensy tweezers and magnifying mirror.

4. Flabby Arms Barbie. Hide Barbie's droopy triceps with these new, roomier-sleeved gowns. Good news on the tummy front too—muumuus with tummy-support panels are included.

5. Bunion Barbie. Years of disco dancing in stiletto heels have definitely taken their toll on Barbie's dainty arched feet. Soothe her sores with the pumice stone and plasters, then slip on soft terry mules.

6. No-more-wrinkles Barbie. Erase those pesky crow's feet and lip lines with a tube of Skin Sparkle-Spackle from Barbie's own line of exclusive age-blasting cosmetics.

7. Soccer Mom Barbie. All that experience as a cheerleader is really paying off as Barbie dusts off her old high school megaphone to root for Babs and Ken, Jr. Comes with minivan in robin-egg blue or white, and cooler filled with doughnut holes and fruit punch.

8. Mid-life Crisis Barbie. It's time to ditch Ken. Barbie needs a change, and Alonzo (her personal trainer) is just what the doctor ordered, along with Prozac. They're hopping in her new red Miata and heading for the Napa Valley to open a B&B. Includes a real tape of "Breaking up is hard to do."

9. Divorced Barbie. Sells for $199.99. Comes with Ken's house, Ken's car, and Ken's boat.

10. Recovery Barbie. Too many parties have finally caught up with the ultimate party girl. Now she does Twelve Steps instead of dance steps. Clean and sober, she's going to meetings religiously. Comes with a little copy of the Big Book and a six-pack of Diet Coke.

11. Post-Menopausal Barbie. This Barbie wets her pants when she sneezes, forgets where she puts things, and cries a lot. She is sick and tired of Ken sitting on the couch watching the tube, clicking through the channels. Comes with Depends and Kleenex. As a bonus this year, the book "Getting In Touch With Your Inner Self" is included.

* * * * * * *

* * * * * * *

*Lord, whatever our circum-
stances or whatever our age,
thank you for helping us to be
of service to others.*

*Believe it or not, you and I can
make a difference as we travel
this journey together.*

* * * * * * *